T0193201

Purpose Pie®

Really Living in the Sweet Spot of Life

Steve Douglas

WESTBOW
PRESS®
A DIVISION OF THOMAS NELSON
& ZONDERVAN

WestBow Press books may be ordered through booksellers or by contacting:

WestBow Press
A Division of Thomas Nelson & Zondervan
1663 Liberty Drive
Bloomington, IN 47403
www.westbowpress.com
1 (866) 928-1240

ISBN: 978-1-5127-0914-8 (sc)
ISBN: 978-1-5127-0915-5 (hc)
ISBN: 978-1-5127-0916-2 (e)

Library of Congress Control Number: 2015913583

Print information available on the last page.

WestBow Press rev. date: 09/23/2015

To the restless souls that know there has to be *more*.

Contents

Author's Note

I am a simple, ordinary man who happens to believe in a God who does complex and extraordinary things through us. By myself I would have never had the talent to create a piece of art like this. I give all credit and adoration to the great Creator for working His masterful artistry within. The only credit I will claim is that I chose to open my heart and listen intently. Once I embraced this intentional and emotional posture, creative ideas flowed to me quickly and often.

If you are already living with purpose, let me be the first to congratulate you. This work will only give added confirmation to the path you are on. If not, then please know that this is not happening by coincidence. *Not hardly!*

This event is happening because of magnificence God desires to come out of you and share with the world. You are about to embark on a Purpose PIE® journey that will empower you to really live in the sweet spot of life—a life of bliss, inner peace, gratitude, and fulfillment.

I am honored to have you share in my experience.

Welcome!

Every man dies, not every man *really* lives.
—William Wallace, Scottish patriot
(1270–1305)

Purpose is the emotional birthplace for
really living and the difference between
just living and *really* living makes all the
difference in the world.
—Steve Douglas

Everything on earth has purpose. Every
disease an herb to cure it and every
person a mission.
—Mourning Dove
Christine Quintasket, writer
(1888–1936)

My Purpose: To honor and love God by
serving and inspiring others
by making a positive and profound
difference in their lives.

My Mission: To be the spark within the flame
by finding the sweet spot of *really*
living for others.

Short Version: Inspiring others to find their voices.

CHAPTER 1

Purpose

Finding one's purpose is a spiritual encounter. Living daily with purpose is a spiritual endeavor that becomes a seed in the rich, fertile ground of creativity. It presents opportunities to nurture and develop something of value and beauty, often from a mere thought or feeling. It welcomes the great Creator to create within. The daily activity is acting out in faith and believing in the unseen. It becomes a springboard in imagining and believing in what could be.

> You were born prepacked. God looked at your entire life, determined your assignment and gave you the tools to do the job. God packed you on purpose for a purpose.
> —Max Lucado, *Cure for the Common Cold*

> The purpose of life is a life of purpose.
> —George Bernard Shaw, writer

Applying one's true, unique, and authentic purpose presses a one-of-a-kind thumbprint on the path to divinity. Yes, a snowflake is beautiful and special—and so are you!

> Since you are like no other being ever created since the
> beginning of time, you are incomparable.
> —Brenda Ueland, writer

For me, finding one's purpose is like coming home for the first and last time: the first time in that this new experience is so surreal and feels different from what you have ever experienced, and the last time in that it feels so magnificent that you will not venture too far from your newfound home of unparalleled significance, indescribable bliss, and unshakable peace.

The last several years our economic environment have produced anxiety and concern for our security and fulfillment in the future. Two basic psychological needs most humans have are feelings of security and a sense of significance, and these times pose a grave threat to both. So many people today feel that something's not right, that something's missing. And guess what? Something very big is missing and causing a sense of emptiness and desperation. In my opinion, never has there been a more critical time for people to discover the purpose God specifically designed for them and then *really* live it!

> Most men lead lives of quiet desperation and go to the
> grave with the song still in them.
> —Henry David Thoreau, writer

Thoreau couldn't make any clearer the profound tragedy of a lack of purpose. But guess what? It doesn't have to be this way. There is not one person I know who is living with purpose and in a state of quiet desperation. What I have observed is when people start to live purposeful lives, they not only start to help and heal others, but they also help and heal themselves in the process. No matter what age you are, what career you have or don't have, or what mistakes you have made, it is not too late to choose to *really* live a magnificent life of purpose.

My interpretation of quiet desperation is that it is an emotional disease. It's been said before that the word *disease* should be hyphenated, as in dis-ease. I see a mind in a state of quiet desperation as a mind that is not at ease, and I see purpose as the restoration and vaccination for the emotional dis-ease of quiet desperation. Purpose is the perfect prescription for the healing of a lack of fulfillment that so many quietly wrestle with.

Suicide takes the lives of nearly thirty thousand Americans every year. I'm confident that if we had the ability to perform an emotional autopsy on all those who have committed suicide, we would discover that not one of them was living with purpose. Suicidal people are consumed by depression and centered on themselves. Purpose-led people are consumed by bliss and centered on contribution to others.

> You can focus on your purpose, or you can focus on your problems. If you focus on your problems, you're going into self-centeredness, which is my problem, my issues, my pain. But one of the easiest ways to get rid of pain is to get your focus off yourself and onto God and others.
>
> —Interview by Paul Bradshaw with Rick Warren,
> author of *Purpose Driven Life*

It is important that people feel a sense of worth. It is also essential that people feel they possess inherent value that is different from others. Living with Purpose PIE® satisfies these desired needs.

For over twenty-five years, my career has been in risk management. From the moment we get out of bed in the morning, we are confronted with risk. Because of my background, I found it very interesting when I first heard about a national survey conducted several years ago on men eighty-five years old and older. They were asked if they could live their lives all over again, what would they do differently. Three similar responses resonated with this insightful group.

1. They would take greater risks.
2. They would reflect more.
3. They would be more involved with something much bigger than themselves.

Do you think there might be some regret for lack of purpose? It sure sounds that way to me.

> We cannot escape fear. We can only transform it into a companion that accompanies us on all our exciting adventures ... Take a risk a day—one small or bold stroke that will make you feel great once you have done it.
>
> —Susan Jeffers, author

I wrote a song that was demoed in Nashville about a man reflecting on his life of disappointment and insignificance. I'd like to share it with you.

Those Sunday Sunset Blues

Here come those heavy feelings again
That wave of dark emotion just keeps rolling in.
I wish I could hide or just run away,
But I'm so afraid it's just here to stay.
It gets me down and feeling empty too.
I feel so helpless ... don't know what to do
In saying good-bye to ...

Those Sunday sunset blues.

See, long ago I had dreams and plans,
Be the master of my fate,
See distant lands.
Had so much I wanted to achieve.
Now it's so hard just to believe.
Lost so much faith,
Don't even have a clue
How to shake ...

Those Sunday sunset blues.

Had so many things I wanted to do,
But life has a way of slip-sliding by you.
Had the greatest intentions,
The best-laid plans,
But come tomorrow morning
That wave of dark emotion
Will rush back in.

Life should be an adventure and so much more,
But in the early morning when I walk out that door
That old familiar ache will rush back in
Of a wasted life and what could've been ... oh ...

Those Sunday sunset blues.

God had planned so much more, but with
All my bad choices and careless mistakes
God only knows if it has sealed my fate.
So I pray above, it's not too late
To wash away, yeah, wash away ...

Those Sunday sunset blues.

The pain was so heavy, I could hardly cope.
I didn't even have one ray of hope.
So I told myself I had to find some inner grit,
Find somehow ... some way ... to get over it.

So I dug real deep, made one last stance.
Fell to my knees on my last chance.
I gave it all to God and put my trust in Him.
Then He held me close and breathed in me
Courage, passion, and purpose too.
He gave me the strength to shake those blues,
Yeah, shake away ...

Those Sunday sunset blues.

It's an amazing thing what hope can do
Now I'm just bustin' with gratitude
'Cause I'm living with inspiration and a new attitude.
So I raise my hands and look to the sky.
Now I've got happy tears as I shout and cry.
Nothing's going to stop me to play out my part
In what God had intended right from the start.
So my heart pitter-patters, my tummy tingles too
'Cause I've got that feeling that I'm all through with ...

Those Sunday sunset blues ... yeah
Those Sunday sunset blues.

The character in this song had a bunch of regrets, but luckily for him, he had the good fortune of having things turn around. Many times when I drop to my knees and surrender all, wonderful things start to happen for me too! In the case of our friend in the song, he trusted God and God delivered. The song ends on a happy, grateful note that's brimming with hope. That's exactly what happens when one discovers God's purpose. Stephen Covey so eloquently called it "living in crescendo," a strong sense and feeling that the best is yet to come. I couldn't agree more!

The man without a purpose is like a ship without a rudder—a waif, a nothing, a no man. Have a purpose in life, and having it throw such strength of mind into your work as God has given you.
—Thomas Carlyle, writer

Just like ships are not to remain in a safe harbor, we were designed not to remain in our safe, familiar comfort zones. I have found that a great emotional tool to help us keep moving forward with purpose is the daily exercise of repeating positive affirmations. One of mine is, "Every day, in every way, by the loving grace of God, I'm blissful, stronger, healthier, wealthier, and my life is full of passion, purpose, peace, and love ... and for this I am grateful."

Affirmations help counter negativity from friends, family, or colleagues and keep you on the path to *really* living in the sweet spot of life. Following are some Purpose PIE® affirmations and principles to give you added clarity and strength in breaking through your safe and familiar comfort zone.

Purpose PIE® Affirmations

1) Purpose is God's will for me.
2) I have been designed with a true, unique, and authentic purpose.
3) Living with purpose heals others and myself.
4) It is healthy for me to nurture my purpose daily.
5) Purpose fills me with bliss, and for this I am grateful.
6) As I listen to my inner voice, I am led to new and exciting discoveries.
7) Living with purpose keeps me in the present, which is a gift.
8) Living with purpose helps me to serve God in a greater capacity.
9) My purpose is always filled with integrity, truth, and love.
10) Living with purpose allows me to play out the divine plan in my life.

Purpose PIE® Principles

1) When we are open to purpose, we open ourselves to trust and faith.
2) Living with purpose is as natural as the air that we breathe.

3) Living with purpose is a daily spiritual experience.

4) As we give our purposes away, we help and heal others and ourselves.

5) Purpose is the antidote to unfulfillment and regret.

6) As we play out our purposes, we move closer to our intended destiny.

7) As we live purposeful lives, we become more creative, hopeful, and expectant.

8) When we choose to live with purpose, we choose to live in our true nature.

9) Purpose feels more like play and less like work, yet you will accomplish more.

10) Living with purpose is an exercise in open-mindedness.

> You are lost the instant you know what the result will be.
>
> —Juan Gris

Just as it took great courage for Lewis and Clark to explore new frontiers, it will take courage for you to explore the vast and limitless frontier of purpose. Always remain open-minded to the wonder of what can be. Start with the first baby step and the next, the next, and so forth. Then one day you will give yourself permission to be okay with stumbling forward into the brave new world of purposeful living. You will find that exploration is generous with priceless gifts to the bold and courageous! So don't concern yourself with the destination but the *journey*. Revel in the experience, and relish each and every moment. Become the exploration extraordinaire that God fully intended you to be. You will be glad you did, and so will the people who cross your path of life.

When you are inspired by some great purpose, some extraordinary project, all your thoughts break bounds. Your mind transcends limitations, your unconsciousness expands in every direction, and you find yourself in a new, great and wonderful world.

—*The Yoga Sutras of Patanjale*

CHAPTER 2

Pie

You may be asking yourself what is PIE, as in Purpose PIE®? It is the sweet spot of purpose. It becomes our daily playground for loving and serving God and others and is an acronym for passion, inspiration, and enthusiasm. Is just the thought of these three words getting you juiced? They do me! I will tell you a fact of life. If you find yourself not living with PIE, then I know something important about you: you are definitely not living with purpose, and I want that to change. Why? Because I've done both, and there is absolutely no comparison to the quality of your precious life once you start to choose to have your daily slice of Purpose PIE®.

> If there is no passion in your life, then have you really
> lived? Find your passion, whatever it may be. Become
> it, and let it become you and you will find great things
> happen For you, To you and Because of you.
> —T. Alan Armstrong, author and writer

Passion is the daily playmate of purpose. They go together like peanut butter and jelly. You will always find them together. They are genuine and lasting friends for life. They move and change the world for the better.

> Passion and purpose go hand in hand. When you discover your purpose, you will normally find it's something you're tremendously passionate about.
>
> —Steve Paulina, blogger and author

Most people love a fresh, homemade pie. But many people, like myself, won't indulge in this simple pleasure too often because of things like calories, trans fat, fat grams, sugar, and cholesterol, to name a few. Well guess what? With Purpose PIE® you don't have to concern yourself with this. You can indulge in it as much as you want to. In fact, just view it as your daily countryside buffet to greatness and not girth!

> Only passions, great passions, can elevate the soul to great things.
>
> —Denis Diderot, French philosopher

I find the word *passion* fascinating in that when I look at the word, there are three other words that pop out at me: *I pass on*. It's interesting because that is exactly what on-fire, passionate people with purpose do. They pass on genuine love, service, and compassion that are as real as it gets. They are consummate contributors to God and mankind. They are always paying it forward and always planting emotional shade trees that they will never sit under. They impact hearts and lives for a lifetime, all because they care. It's been said that people don't care about how much you know until they know how much you care. Purpose-led people are very passionate about passing on care to others.

They may forget what you said, but never forget how
you made them feel.
—Carl W. Buechner, author

Years ago when I discovered God's purpose for my life, I was blessed with a eureka moment. Shortly after I started living with purpose, I became intrigued with how the words *inspiration* and *motivation* were used interchangeably. Over and over again the sports and corporate worlds make reference to these words as being similar. Even in casual conversation with a friend, neighbor, or relative, the same rule generally applies. But after much study and reflection, it came to me why these two words cause confusion and create a false sense of perception. Please let me state something before we go any further: Purpose PIE® has absolutely *nothing* to do with motivation. Surprised? I was at first. But now I understand this distinction with great clarity. It is important for you to understand it fully as well. The confusion comes in because they have one distinct similarity: they both attain results. Typically, highly self-motivated and inspired people have been able to attain enormous results, especially when they are focused and very intentional. But after the "results" similarity, they are as opposite as night and day. Let me explain.

Inspiration is derived from the Latin word *inspirare*, meaning to breathe life into another. The *American Heritage Dictionary* describes inspire this way: To affect, guide, or arouse by divine influence. The *Merriam-Webster Dictionary* describes inspiration this way: "A divine influence or action on a person believed to qualify him or her to receive and communicate sacred revelation." Pretty neat stuff, huh? Here comes the great distinction! According to the *Collins English Dictionary,* self-motivation is defined this way: "motivated or driven by oneself or one's own desire, without any external agency."

The word *motivation* derives from the Latin verb *movere,* meaning to move. For example, it is what moves a person to make certain choices, to engage in action, and to expend effort and persist in action. Through the years there has been considerable debate and disagreement among scholars with regard to the theory and mechanics of motivation. Over the years I have observed a myriad of different words that describe the motivation process—words like *induce, insight, provoke, instigate, bias, sway, tempt, seduce, bribe, enforce, impel, propel, whip, lash,* and *goad.* Other than the "results" similarity, are you starting to see the contrast? In my opinion, I see motivation and inspiration like this: motivation's birthplace comes from the mind of man and is derived and sustained by the ego. It's been said before ego is an acronym *edging God out.* You get the drift. Ego-driven people have it their way. God is not only left out of their pictures of daily activity, but He is also left out of their hearts.

On the other hand, inspiration's birthplace comes from the heart of man and is derived and sustained by the Spirit. With this thought in mind, I created an acronym for spirit: *spiritually partnering in relational intimacy together.* You are choosing to open your mind and your heart and inviting the Holy Spirit to join you in a very intimate and personal way. You create a bond, friendship, and love that becomes indescribable and priceless. You start to make an impact in the world as never before, all because you have opened your heart to receiving love and a whole lot of help. So what is it to be—love and help or no love and help? As for me, I'm sticking with love and help. You see, when you choose to open your heart's door to love and help, you are taking your first baby steps into *really* living. This is a promise! Once you take that very first step, there will be no going back. Remember when I talked earlier about coming home for the first and last time? After you take those first few steps, you'll know exactly what I'm talking about. It brings me bliss just thinking about the life-changing experience that is waiting for you.

I see the motivated, ego-driven person as a sole proprietor who is having it his way but at the expense of taking on way too much risk. Remember—I've been specializing in risk management for over twenty-five years. So my question to you is, why take on all that unnecessary risk when you don't have to? My strong advice to you would be to choose to live an inspired, Spirit-led, and purpose-fed life. I see the inspired, Spirit-led person as one who is in a *soul*-partnership. These people are not only receiving a whole lot of help, but it also comes with a lot less risk. Sound better? It sure does to me.

When you boil it all down, motivation comes from man and the wants and will of man. Inspiration comes from God being invited and welcomed to work through man. When you choose to partner with God, you will be filled with noble and reverent emotion that will enlighten and empower you beyond your wildest imagination. Remember, my mission—to be the spark within the flame in finding the sweet spot of *really* living for others. Won't you join me, the Purpose PIE® guy, in *really* living a life of fulfillment and magnificence? If you do, I will promise you this: you will thank me for it—but you will thank God more!

> Before you can inspire with emotion, you must be swamped with it yourself. Before you can move their tears, your own must follow. To convince them, you must yourself believe.
> —Winston Churchill, British prime minister

I have seen motivation referred to as "an impulse to inspire." I find this interesting because motivation takes on an initial outward appearance of inspiration, as we discussed earlier, in that they both attain results. But there's a pretty big difference between having an impulse to do push-ups and plank exercises and actually doing them.

I'm not too invested when I have just an impulse to do something. When you dig a little deeper, though, you will discover that initial outward similarity is pretty different after all. It's kind of like comparing lightning to a lightning bug. While one may bug you (no pun intended), the other can kill you! Motivation- and inspiration-led people are always doing things and gaining results. But the difference is in why they are doing it. Motivated people are in it for themselves— the me, myself, and I syndrome. The inspired soul is doing it first and foremost for God and others. This is where a paradox comes rushing in. It's the old give-and-receive principle that has been with us since the beginning of time. No matter how giving and serving a person is in his or her true nature, God is going to always give back ... *more!* He will give things like bliss, inner peace, and fulfillment. You can't buy any of these, but if you had to put a price tag on them, they all would be priceless.

> An interior man will make impressions on hearts by a single word animated by the Spirit of God, than another, by a whole discourse which has cost, him much labor and in which he has exhausted all his power of reasoning.
>
> —Louis Lallement, 1587–1635

Because of everything mentioned, I see motivation as very deceptive in nature and consider it an imposter to inspiration. When you think about it on a deeper level, motivation can't even hold a candle to inspiration, because it doesn't have the spiritual authenticity.

> The lamp of the Lord searches the spirit of a man; it searches out his inmost being. (Proverbs 20:27 NIV)

Inspiration comes from the truth as it originates from the one that creates truth. This truth has always been and will always be steadfast and consistent. Inspiration becomes an intentional life path of love-filled consistencies of servanthood and contribution to God and mankind. Motivation manifests a life path of consistent inconsistencies with God and our fellow man. Inspiration is authentic and genuine as it is driven by spiritual purpose. Motivation is a pretender as it is always driven by a personal agenda.

> Firmness of purpose is one of the most necessary sinews of character, and one of the best instruments of success. Without it, genius wastes its efforts in a maze of inconsistencies.
> —Lord Chesterfield

I view one living a purposeless life as a great pretender. I say this because these people are not doing what they were designed to do, be, and become. For many years I identified surrender with weakness. What I found to be true, however, is that in surrender lies our greatest strength. We start to receive *help* that is immeasurably more than we could ever ask for or imagine. Surrender doesn't disempower. Surrender empowers and takes one to new heights. It doesn't debilitate but liberates and sets one free. A daily life surrendered to inspiration generates the spark to set our spirits aglow.

> The most powerful weapon on earth is the human spirit on fire.
> —Marshal Ferdinand Foch

Another common trait of highly motivated people is that they compare and compete against others. In this type of lifestyle, the emotional highs are temporary and short-lived as the mind (ego) is constantly searching and never fully satisfied with achievement. Achievement has a beginning and an end. It takes on an inner spin of unfulfillment and ongoing restlessness.

The inspired soul that is being led by Purpose PIE® feels very comfortable and satisfied in his or her pie crust or skin! The reason these people are at ease with inner peace is their lifestyles are not about achievement but contribution. They don't compare and compete, as they are abundance thinkers. They always feel an afterglow because of the accomplishment of others. They emotionally applaud and rejoice in others' success. They feel there is plenty of PIE to go around. They don't fall into the scarcity mind-set lie. They see their contributions as long lasting and enduring as they have forgotten about themselves in the bliss of servanthood. And as they learn to forget themselves on their Purpose PIE® path, they start to know themselves for the first time.

In my life I've learned that goals are great, but start with your heart before you live and give your part. By choosing to trust inspiration, you will replace grunting, groaning, and speed bumps with hooting, hollering, and goose bumps. Choose to have your perspiration (your life's work) come from your inspiration and not motivation so that you may put an end to a life of quiet desperation.

Thoughts on Motivation and Inspiration

Motivation	Inspiration
Ego/me myself and I	Spirit/God and others driven
Competes with others	Completes others
Inner restlessness	Inner peace
Making a dollar	Making a difference
Fumbles through life	Is humble in life

Takes credit for achievements	Credits God for contributions
Pretender	Surrender
Gains from relationships	Gives to relationships

Two men who led daily lives of inspiration were the great composer Bach and the popular writer C. S. Lewis. It was noted that at the end of Bach's compositions, he would write the initials SDG—*Soli Deo Gloria*, which means, "To God alone be the glory."

One of my favorite quotes by the great C. S. Lewis was on humility: "Humility is not thinking less of yourself, it's thinking of yourself less."

To eat humble pie, in common usage, is to apologize and face humiliation for a serious error. Why risk putting oneself in a potential regretful and embarrassing moment by the continual pursuit of the ego-driven life? I say surrender that pretender to a daily slice of Purpose PIE®. Stay humble and grateful in a daily inspirational mind-set. Let your spirit partner with you and take you into a realm of peace and empowerment like you have never experienced.

The third part of our better than a blue ribbon–winning pie is E, enthusiasm. Enthusiasm comes from two Greek words, *En* and *Theos*, meaning in God, within God, or inspired by God.

> Enthusiasm is the divine particle in our composition:
> With it we are great, generous and true; without it, we
> are little, false and mean.
>
> —Letitia Landon, poet

I don't know if I necessarily believe that lack of enthusiasm promotes meanness per se, but I sure have seen a ton of unenthusiastic people in my life who are about as lifeless as it gets! And it all makes sense. They're not *really* living. They are wandering aimlessly in that sad state of quiet desperation.

> Nothing great was ever accomplished without
> enthusiasm.
>
> —Ralph Waldo Emerson

When I was growing up as a little boy in West Palm Beach, Florida, my parents' motto was to work hard and play hard and do it with enthusiasm! One weekend while working in the yard with my dad, I became very unenthusiastic about the way one of our conversations was going. It went something like this: "Hey, Dad, you know next year I'm going to be sixteen?"

My dad, still raking the grass, answered, "I know that."

"Hey, Dad, did you know that when I turn sixteen and get my driver's license, then I can drive a car?"

My dad, still raking, answered, "Yeah, I know that too."

"Hey, Dad, when I turn sixteen and get my driver's license, are you and Mom going to buy me a new car?"

My dad kept raking but now looked at me for the first time and didn't say a word, which prompted my next hopeful but concerned question. "Hey, Dad, how about a used car?"

My dad stopped raking and had a very serious look on his face. For the first time it started to set in that he was not as enthusiastic about this car thing as I was. And then he became this all-powerful weather forecaster who was forecasting dark skies and heavy winds and rain on the very day of my car parade. Can you believe it?

I know I sure didn't want to when he said, "Steve, do you have two arms, two legs, and a brain?"

I answered respectfully but was becoming extremely worried about where this conversation was going. Looking at my dad, I answered, "Yes, sir!"

To that he replied, "Then you figure out how to get one."

Starting to finally realize that this weather forecast appeared to be pretty accurate, I asked, "Are you serious?"

Still not raking he answered, "As serious as a heart attack."

Right then and there in that defining moment of my life, I knew I had better find a way to devise a plan with enormous enthusiasm or this car dream thing was coming to a screeching halt! At the time it seemed like the world was coming to an end, but in truth a very valuable life lesson was about to unfold. An enthusiastic work ethic seed had been planted, and the future harvest was to be nothing short of priceless!

> Pray as everything depended on God. Work as though everything depended on you.
>
> —Saint Augustine

> The only place success comes before work is in the dictionary.
>
> —Author, unknown

Move forward a few weeks, and in the late afternoon, I was playing football with a bunch of my neighborhood friends in this large, open field. Our play field was owned by Mr. Johnson, a very quiet widower who stayed to himself. As we finished a play, we realized Mr. Johnson was standing next to us. He wanted to know if any of us wanted to do some heavy yard work for the next couple of days. He stated that he needed three boys. No sooner had he said this than my hand enthusiastically went up into the air, waving with passion, as I sensed this could be a key opportunity to the keys of my desired car. Then we heard him say as he pointed, "I'll take you, you, and you." Luckily I was one of the "yous," as well as my friends Eddie and Ricky.

He basically said that he needed us to be at his house the next two days, shortly after sunrise, and we should expect to work up to dark. There was no mention of the work duties or the pay offered to get the job done. This was more than fine with me, as I wanted a car and I had to start somewhere. Mr. Johnson's house sat on several acres, and over the next couple of days, we found ourselves cutting grass (push mowers), edging, raking, trimming hedges, etc. It wasn't too long into this task that it became rather obvious to me that all three of us had a very different viewpoint on how work should be performed. Even though I was aware of the obvious, I still continued at the pace I initially started.

After two long days of physical work, right before sunset, Mr. Johnson invited us into his home. All three of us were filthy and drenched with sweat. As he led us through his house, he took us into a room with a table that had three large glasses of ice water and stacks of one-dollar bills on it. At this point I really didn't know what to expect, other than I now thought I could maybe hear the gentle purr of my car's engine.

What happened next was truly one of my greatest life lessons. As Mr. Johnson asked Eddie to come and receive his stack of dollar bills, Eddie's face was beaming. The excitement was written all over his face—that is until Mr. Johnson called Ricky and we discovered he had taken it upon himself to reward Ricky with 25 percent more in dollar bills. Eddie's facial expression went down like the setting sun, just like outside of the room we were standing in. All of a sudden, that bright, cheery smile started to fade into disappointment and regret. I sensed that the stack of bills in Eddie's hand was beginning to lose some of its luster. We all were assigned the exact same task for the same allotted time.

Mr. Johnson's next words took me on an unexpected trip and greater distance than any car has or could ever take me. He was about to validate and confirm one of my parents' mantras. When you play, play hard, and when you work, work hard and do it with enthusiasm! As Mr. Johnson called my name, I walked toward him with nervous anticipation, and then he presented me with one of the greatest gifts I have ever received in my life. He said, "Boys, these two days you worked for me, I was observing you many times from inside my home. Eddie, you did a nice job, and I thank you for your effort. Ricky, you put forth a greater effort, and I have rewarded you accordingly. Steve, you worked with enthusiasm, and I want you to come and work for me, if you would like to." And then I thought, *If I'd like to? Are you kidding me?* At that very moment, I could almost hear my car pulling out of the driveway. By the way, the stack of bills that Mr. Johnson gave me was 50 percent more than Eddie's stack. Now Eddie's face was taking on a hue of someone in the first stage of food poisoning.

I worked for Mr. Johnson for several years, after school, on weekends, and during summers. He was a wonderful and generous employer and even better mentor and life guide. I am convinced that God placed Mr. Johnson on my path for a reason. I sure felt that way the very first time I pulled my two-tone 1964 Chevy II that I paid cash for out of my driveway. What a life lesson. What a moment to remember. What a high!

> The real secret of success is enthusiasm.
> —Walter Chrysler, auto executive

> Enthusiasm is the most important thing in life.
> —Tennessee Williams, dramatist

> A man can succeed at almost anything for which he has unlimited enthusiasm.
> —Charles M. Schwab, steel executive

> Enthusiasm is an ever flowing energy extravaganza
> that takes you right to a bonanza.
> —Steve Douglas, Purpose PIE® guy

When people with purpose sit at the table of life and enthusiastically feast upon their Purpose PIE®, it will do far more than just please their palates. It will fortify their bodies, minds, and spirits, as well as impact many that happen to cross their paths of life.

Purpose PIE®
Steve Douglas

Life is short,
so I'm telling you why,
before you die
you need to live
with *Purpose PIE®*

I've had cherry
and blueberry too
and apple, peach, and pumpkin, just to name a few.
But now I know
the sweetest pie for you
is filled with purpose
through and through.
'Cause inside that crust
you can trust
three new gifts
just waiting for you.

Once I was blind
but now I see,
this ain't any plain-old
P-I-E.
For the *P* stands for passion
that will fill you up.
The *I* will inspire
and set you on fire,
the *E* will enthuse
so you can't lose
all of that potential
that's been lying in you.

And when your purpose
flows through you,
it will change your life.
It will change you too.
Now there's nothing in the world
that you can't do.

Cause you're flying like a kite
so high in the sky.
You're soaring like a bird
and free as the wind
you're touching the world in a different way.
When you ask this question
and then you say,
Why am I here
on Mother Earth?
Then your voice inside
will kindly oblige.

It will soften your heart
and become your guide.
You'll be filled with passion.
Deep inside
inspiration will
become your ride.
Enthusiasm you
can no longer hide.
Every man dies
not every man lives.
With *Purpose PIE®*
you'll *really* live.
'Cause you'll no longer take
but give and give.

Now you have a new attitude
'cause you're filled with such gratitude
just knowing that God
breathed new life into you.
He's filled you up
with passion
inspiration
and enthusiasm too!

And when your days
are coming to an end
you'll have no regrets,
for this message you did send
to a hurting world
that was empty too.

You gave it hope;
you gave it you.

Now the world
is a better place
'cause *Purpose PIE*®
filled that hollow space
not just for you
but the human race.

That quite desperation
that's been locked inside,
you'll count your lucky stars
the moment that it dies

Before you say
your final good-bye
you'll want to thank
your *Purpose PIE*®
because you really lived in such a way.
You flew like a kite
so high in the sky.
You soared like a bird
and were as free as the wind.
You touched the world
in a different way.

And now there's nothing
left to say,
so I thank You, God,
and I'll leave it this way.

Steve Douglas

I'm so grateful.
I'm no longer blue,
and I pray the same for you.

Now it's your turn.
Why don't you have a slice
and put an end
to all this stress and strife?
Then you'll know
what I mean
when I say ...

Me oh my,
what a life I've had
with Purpose PIE®.
I didn't have to die
so lost and empty
deep inside.
Me oh my,
my *Purpose PIE®*,
me oh my,
what a high!
Me oh my,
my sweet and wonderful *Purpose PIE®!*

CHAPTER 3

Inner Voice

For me, the very first step I took on my Purpose PIE® path was prompted by a statement I read in a professional sales book. This statement not only resonated with me, but it also shook me to the very core. The author stated that he felt the greatest deterrent to creating excellence in one's life was a lack of purpose. For the very first time, I questioned what my purpose was and became very intentional in discovering it. Why was I truly here in this moment in time? What were my unique gifts that I was supposed to share with the world? How was I to go about uncovering this all-important, life-changing thing called purpose?

I came to the conclusion that I would find the answer to all these questions through prayer. And pray I did! I spent days, weeks, and several months of sincere heartfelt prayer. All the while I had no earthly idea of how this eventual enlightenment was to present itself. That was until my wife and I were vacationing in Banff, Canada. One night I became restless at 2:30 a.m. and decided to get up and go into the next room so I wouldn't disturb Patti, my wife. I made a pot of coffee, got a notepad and pen in hand, and then nestled into the still, early morning quiet.

> Call to me and I will answer you and tell you great and
> unsearchable things you do not know. (Jeremiah 33:3 NIV)

After many minutes of prayer and reflection, I picked up my pen and wrote a statement that would have far-reaching ramifications for my life going forward. That statement was: "My purpose is to serve and to inspire by making a positive and profound difference in the lives of others." Since that memorable early morning, my purpose has evolved into this: "My purpose is to honor and love God by serving and inspiring others by making a positive and profound difference in their lives."

> Learn to get in touch with the silence within yourself,
> and know that everything in this life has a purpose.
> —Elizabeth Kubler-Ross

So, what is your life's purpose? Are you ready to start exploring the journey to greatness, fulfillment, and passion like you've never experienced before? Then choose to find a place where you can become still and quiet. Become very sincere and intentional in asking questions to your inner voice.

> You will seek me and find me when you seek me with
> all your heart. (Jeremiah 29:11–13 NIV)

And when the time is right, your inner voice will speak to you. Here is a little insight for you: your inner voice will not communicate with you through words but by feelings and deep emotions. Be prepared to experience an encounter of numinous beauty. You will be filled with a sense of the presence of divinity. Remember the acronym for EGO— Edging God Out? When you choose to communicate with your inner voice, you are detaching yourself from the ego and welcoming *spirit*. Remember my acronym for spirit: Spiritually Partnering In Relational Intimacy Together.

You have now entered into a holy relationship that will provide for you a continuous flow of answers, guidance, and help. In M. Scott Peck's classic book *The Road Less Traveled*, the very first sentence of the book starts out like this: "Life is difficult." What great truth. So why not ask for help? I do every day, and I recommend the same for you. It won't make your life perfect, but it will become much less difficult and far more rewarding. Remember, God is a God of free will, so it is up to us to take that first step.

> When a man takes one step toward God, God takes more steps toward that man than there are sands in the worlds of time.
>
> —The Work of the Charist

> God wants only one thing in the Whole World, the thing which it needs; ... that thing is to find the innermost part of the noble spirit of man clean and ready for Him to accomplish the divine purpose therein. He has all the power in heaven and earth, but the power to do His work in man against man's will he has not got.
>
> —John Tauler, 1304–1361

When you truly seek God's divine purpose that He specifically designed for you, you will receive it. And know fully, that this is not a once-and-for-all situation. This is not an end point. This is a starting point. You will experience an ebb and flow of emotions prompted by fresh new insight. The endless chatter and noise of life takes its place as a faint echo in the background. (More on the voice of chatter in chapter 7.) You will also notice that you don't expend near the energy that you used to with others' opinions. Seeking approval of others also is not nearly as important. Your new life path is taking a fork in the road to pleasing God. What a wonderful trade you have made—unfulfillment for fulfillment, inner turmoil for inner peace, and chatter for what really matters.

> Don't let the noise of other's opinions drown out your
> inner voice.
> —Steve Jobs, Apple cofounder

Think of this journey that you are on as a daily spiritual encounter. You become very intentional in your intimate, spiritual relationship in seeking *guidance*: you Give Up Independent Demeanor And Now Choose Enlightenment. You begin to gladly give up your low-hanging ceilings for limitless possibilities. You become tidal. You empty yourself to fill yourself. You carve out time to converse with God Almighty.

> There is not in the world a kind of life more sweet
> and delightful than that with a continual conversation
> with God.
> —Brother Lawerence, *The Practice of the Presence of God*

Are you starting to see the pattern here? Ask, listen, receive ... ask, listen, receive ...

> All you need to do to receive guidance is to ask for it
> and then listen.
> —Sanaya Roman

Trust that still, small voice that says, this might work
and I'll try it!

—Diane Mariechild

I love Jesus's interpretation and explanation comparing the wind
to everyone born of the Spirit.

The wind blows wherever it pleases. You hear its sound,
but you cannot tell where it comes from or where it is
going. So it is with everyone born of the Spirit. (John
3:8 NIV)

No, we can't see the wind, and we certainly don't know where it
comes from or where it's going. We can say the same thing about our
inner spirit. But this doesn't prevent you or me from feeling it. The
wind comes and goes as it pleases. The Spirit loves and responds to the
invitation of an open heart.

My prayer of prayers is for you right now, at this very moment, is
to invite your inner voice to come and be in intimate relationship with
you. In that perfect moment when it shares God's divine purpose made
just for you, may your emotional sails be filled with winds of the Spirit
that will take you to new discoveries that you weren't even capable of
asking for or imagining.

Amen.

My Friend That I Can't See

Lyrics by: Steve Douglas

When lost for words, need answers too
When life's gone crazy, without a clue
I get still and quiet as I search for you
Then you shine your light, your light on truth

You're my Friend I feel, but I can't see
Feel You in my heart, just waitin' on me
You never bother or interrupt
You're always waitin', just to hear my stuff

You're, so much more than I deserve
You're not like life in throwin' curves
Feelings are how You speak to me
Feel You best when I'm on my knees

You're my friend I feel, but I can't see
Feel You in my heart, just waitin' on me
You never bother or interrupt
You're always waitin', just to hear my stuff

You're like the wind as You come and go
As You fill my sails, yeah, this I know
I was stumbling in the dark, but now I see
There's a perfect love, just stirrin' in me
Yeah, a perfect love … just stirrin' … in me

CHAPTER 4

Numinous Nutrition

From the very moment we come into the world, we all need one thing to survive. We are dependent on our mother's milk or for someone to go to the store and buy some baby formula for us! Spiritual nutrition is later needed or we may very well die on the inside. We all need spiritual nutrition, whether we want to admit it or not. *Numinous* is an English adjective describing the presence of a divinity. The numinous experience also has a personal quality to it, in that the person feels like he or she is in communion with a *wholly other*. It also has been described as being supernatural, mysterious, and holy.

> Think of yourself as an incandescent power, illuminated and perhaps forever talked to by God and his messengers.
>
> —Brenda Ueland

We all have been blessed with spiritual gifts. However, many choose to use them on a limited basis or not at all. God truly activates our spiritual gifts when we choose to open our minds and hearts and genuinely invite this experience to be manifested.

> There are different kinds of gifts, but the same Spirit.
> There are different kinds of service, but the same Lord.
> There are different kinds of working, but the same God
> works all of them in all men. (1 Corinthians 12:4–6 NIV)

So, my dear reader, let me say to you with deep sincerity: *namaste.* For those of you not familiar with this scared greeting, it translates as, "I salute the divine within you; I salute your God-given gifts." And how do you know when your gifts are activated and being utilized to the fullest? When you find yourself on your Purpose PIE® path of a purpose-filled life that is chock full with passion, inspiration, and enthusiasm.

Not quite there yet? Then press on. We all have an abundance of help just around the corner. It's okay to finally admit our dependence on God. In fact, it becomes a very liberating moment when you realize you're ready to have life work through you in place of always having to work on life. The payoff? It's far more rewarding with far less expended energy. All you need is a little faith. Faith is choosing to believe in the unseen. The pinnacle of faith is not *asking* for a desired outcome but rather *thanking* God in advance, as if it has already happened. Then you experience what I call "relational empowerment." You get *help*! And the *help* you receive is beyond comparison or measure. But with this *help* comes what I call a responsibility to possibility. We have to raise our inner emotional bar of what can be. Because of the unfamiliarity, it becomes scary for most. I say it's okay to feel the fear, just breathe deep, say a prayer, and do it anyway. You will now be taking the first step toward your rightful destiny.

> Our deepest fear is not that we are inadequate. Our
> deepest fear is that we are powerful beyond measure.
> —Marianne Williamson

Remember a couple of things when it comes to possibility thinking. It's okay to place ceilings on your potential but not on God's as He is working through you. When you picture God working through you, just imagine an open, endless blue sky.

> The jig, in short, is up: God knows that the sky's the limit. Anyone honest will tell you that possibility is far more frightening than impossibility, that freedom is far more terrifying than any prison. If we do, in fact, have to deal with a force beyond ourselves that involves itself in our lives, then we may have to move into action on previously impossible dreams.
>
> —Julia Cameron, *The Artist's Way*

Yeah, responsibility to possibility. When we operate of the spirit, wo fall in the rank of Spiritually Partnering In Relational Intimacy Together. And as we partner with God in the realm of possibility, we have our part to deliver on. We ask, we listen, and as God feeds us numinous nutrition (spiritual food), we take action accordingly. We begin to fulfill our duty of responsibility to possibility. We act in moving forward. When we ACT^3 upon God's whispers, we witness firsthand Action Creating Traction To Takeoff.

We finally begin the liftoff toward the ultimate accomplishment of finishing God's divine will for us.

> My food is to do the will of Him who sent me and to finish His work. (John 4:34 NIV)

As we grow weary of our ongoing talking the talk, we become bold through God's spiritual sustenance as we take action. It is that very ACT^3 alone that lifts us off of our very safe yet desolate someday isle (someday I'll). We all know about someday isle. Someday I'll go back to college to get my education. Someday I'll do my share and get involved with community service. Someday I'll pay the price to discover my true calling and carry it out to completion. Someday I'll ... and the beat goes on and on and on.

Let me be perfectly honest with you. Purpose PIE® has been something I've been flirting with for ten-plus years. Together we were washed up on the empty beach of someday isle. Just talking the talk. Just some good old pie-in-the-sky baloney. So what big ol' phony baloney do you have stuck way up high in a coconut tree on someday isle? If I can do this responsibility to possibility life change, so can you! You know why? It's because of the fact that with God all things are possible! So what's been tugging at your heartstrings? To this, I say *creatio ex nihilo*, meaning creation out of nothing. What fancy have you been flirting with that, given the chance, you would love to share with the world? What mustard seed of a thought have you been playing with and have mistakenly put it back in your play box?

> We don't stop playing because we get old; we grow old because we stop playing.
>
> —George Bernard Shaw

> Creativity is ... seeing something that doesn't exist already. You need to find out how you can bring it into being and that way be a playmate with God.
>
> —Michele Shea

Here's the deal. As you arrive closer to your purpose and start to share it with others, you will discover that it doesn't feel like work, but play.

The masters in the art of living make little distinction between their work and their play, their labor and their leisure, their minds and their bodies, their information, their recreation, their love and their religion. They hardly know which is which; they simply pursue their vision of excellence at whatever they do, leaving others to decide whether they are working or playing.

—James A Michener

Purpose PIE® lives in a state of paradox, with serious questions, listening, and receiving. This all leads to serious servanthood, contribution, and accomplishment. Here's the funny twist. All of this is manifested out of serious play with the master playmate of one's purpose. New to this playground of life, one might ask, "Can it really be this much fun?" The resounding answer is yes. Yes, it can!

We need to commit to a lifelong mind-set to remember God (*memoria Dei*). In this commitment we need to be sensitive and pay attention to what the Spirit is saying to us daily. Numinous nutrition is all around us. It is our duty to develop a keen awareness of not what we are in lack of per se but that our empty inner well of possibility can be filled in the blink of one's eye. We need to remain on high alert when we are asking, seeking, and knocking on God's door. For many times we may receive a Godwink, as that door may open when we least expect it.

For me, a Godwink is all about God Opens Doors When I Nurture Knocking. When I take responsibility to *ACT^3* in the development and cultivating of knocking on God's door, then many times this will open the floodgates to the river of numinous nutrition that will fill our empty and parched emotional well. We become keenly aware of coincidences as they begin to happen with greater regularity and more profound impact.

> Coincidences are God's way of remaining anonymous.
> —Albert Einstein

> The Lord will guide you always; he will satisfy your needs in a sun-scorched land and will strengthen your frame. You will be like a well-watered garden, like a spring whose waters never fail. (Isaiah 58:11 NIV)

In all relationships the phone rings both ways, just as both doors may be knocked upon. In Warner Sallman's famous painting *Christ at Heart's Door*, we discover that there is no outside knob or latch on the door. This indicates that one must open one's heart to Christ within, as He will not force His way inside. From this I have learned a great and wonderful truth in life. Once we choose to authentically open our hearts' doors to His loving knock, then we become transformed as we now yearn to knock on His door daily. We want our numinous nutrition. We want our daily bread. This heartfelt change of voluntary discipline (knocking on His door) in turn leads to involuntary transmutation (a spiritual hunger being satisfied within). It is here where we nurture the receiving and giving of that sacred knock where the heart's door begins to open to extraordinary possibilities. It is here where we begin to SLAY unfulfillment, mediocrity, and a boatload of other junk that we no longer want to carry with us.

S—Surrender to His will.
L—Listen to His voice.
A—ACT^3 out our calling/purpose.
Y—Yearn for more of the same for ourselves and for others.

We see clearly now what this *BREAD* from heaven is all about:

> Believing—we *really* can do the task He has given us.
> Reassuring—we can have boundless hope doing God's will.
> Encouraging—He encourages us to move forward as He stirs within.
> Assisting—He's always there with Godwinks along the way.
> Delivering—He will deliver the goods to our inner spiritual hunger.

He will one day deliver us to a glorious conclusion. This BREAD tastes so good it's like eating dessert. And guess what? There's more than enough for everyone. And this takes us to a state of gratitude the likes of which we have never felt.

CHAPTER 5

Gratitude

Okay then, my Purpose PIE® friend. We are now witnessing and experiencing firsthand that our path of discovery of our true, unique, and authentic purpose has a rhythm and flow to it. We ask questions to our inner voice, listen intently, and learn to become very sensitive to the help we receive in the form of numinous nutrition and Godwinks. As we venture further down this path of spiritual discovery, we start to sense that just maybe this *really* is our natural and designed birthright. We also start to understand that our inner doubting Thomas (more on this later) who has stymied us from living out our dreams is nothing more than misplaced fear and an illusion. When this newfound truth starts to permeate our hearts and spirits, we start to see the world in a different light. We start to travel lighter as we invite the light to travel within. Any guardedness, skepticism, and cynicism start to dissipate. We begin to realize the beauty and empowerment that is manifested from the daily communion with our inner voice.

> But the Counselor, the Holy Spirit, whom the Father will send in my name, will teach you all things and will remind you of everything I have said to you. (John 14:26 NIV)

I myself do nothing. The Holy Spirit accomplishes all
through me.

—William Blake, author

And as we evolve and grow further, we see that God has designed
not just a generalized purpose for us but a personalized, specific
purpose within our purposes, so to speak—a mission, a calling,
an OBT (one big thing), a Purpose PIE®, if you will. It's kind of like
differentiation between a snowflake and a snowstorm or a thumbprint
and a thumbtack. We each have been created and designed with our
responsibility to possibility to find out what it is.

When we pray, we talk to God and have an opportunity to exercise
a beautiful privilege. Praying should never be viewed as a duty,
especially when we have the blessing to be able to address any concern
or question we may have at any time. When we meditate, God talks to
us, and this too is a glorious privilege.

Listen to God in silence when we have spoken to Him,
for he speaks in His turn during prayer.

—John Peter deCaussade

The more we find ourselves in communion with God, the closer
we will come in the discovery of His calling to the specific mission
within our life. And as God's calling to our life mission becomes
clearer, we will witness an unfolding of our creative spirit as we
stumble forward. We find ourselves fulfilling our designed function
to be co-creators with our Creator. We will find the partnering within
our spirit is taking full bloom. And because of this, we can no longer
take credit for our creative endeavors. We realize that our limitless
imagination and artistic ingenuity are coming from somewhere
other than ourselves. I love the word *creative* and all the beauty it so

magically and graciously gives birth to. For me, the word *CREATIVE* is all about:

- Cultivating
- Rare
- Experiences
- After
- Trusting
- Inner
- Voice
- Expressions

> Within the man, God has placed a divine seed. A seed of his self. The God of might had created the earth's mightiest. The Creator had created, not a creature, but another creator. And the One who had chosen to love had created one who could love in return.
>
> —*In the Eye of the Storm*

And the rarest and most glorious experience any of us could ever hope for is when we once and for all, genuinely connect on the depth of God's call to love. God's calling to each and every one of us is a true call to love. Think about it. God's first and greatest commandment is, "Love the Lord your God with all your heart and with all your soul and all your mind. And the second commandment is like it: Love your neighbor as yourself." For me, God's *CALLING* for each of us is all about: Creating A Labor Love Inspired Near God.

Everything we labor in should be in a labor of love. Worshipping and honoring God, our families, our relationships, our purposes, and anything and everything under the sun should be done with a labor of love. That's why it is so vitally important not to just trudge through life with a mundane job but to *really* live and love the playing out of your daring dreams. Don't just have a career but carry out your calling in loving and fulfilling the mission God has crafted just for you.

Don't get me wrong. I'm not saying a chosen career is bad for you per se, as I've had two great ones in my life. But what I am saying is that it will be in our very best interest if we can somehow transition into the sweet spot of our life missions before we die. Yes, we all have duties and responsibilities to do in order to provide an income to sustain ourselves and our families. But here's the deal. I don't care how much income you ever generate from a career, how many awards you win, how many benefits and perks you have, how much recognition you receive or applause that you garner from the world. At the end of the day, at the end of your life, if you're *really* honest with yourself, you will know full well that something may still be missing. And that something missing is the loss of the pinnacle of the labor of love. It's the tragic loss of not spiritually partnering in relational intimacy with God. It's the lost opportunity to *really* live in the sweet spot of a one-of-a-kind mission that God personally designed and created just for you. The way I see it, when people start to move forward with their God-ordained MISSION, they will then experience this: My Inspirational Sweet Spot Is Opening Now!

One will no longer want to remain in a tight bud, which has been holding all of their beauty and magnificence within.

> And the time came when the risk to remain tight in a
> bud was more painful than the risk it took to blossom.
> —Anais Nin

One will now sense it is time to blossom and to flower into the warm, inviting, and radiant light of God's perfect love. The way I see it, the unfolding of one's magnificence is this: At one time or another, we all are a *BUD*—Beauty Under Darkness.

So much greatness that God has gifted each and every one of us has been lying in the dark, closed and hidden from the world to see and enjoy. And then one day we feel led to evolve, stretch, and grow as we BLOSSOM: Believing Life Offers Sweet Spots of Magnificence. As this newfound sensation builds, we find ourselves opening more and more as we are drawn to God's loving light. Then one day we FLOWER: Find Love Opening With Every Ray. Then we find ourselves deeply rooted in God's magnificent garden of what can be!

> Cracks of Light ... the human soul is to God is as the flower to the sun; it opens at its approach, and shuts when it withdraws.
>
> —Benjamin Whichcote

As we choose to draw closer and closer to our source, our great Creator who creates within leaves His calling card of efflorescence upon us, we experience a gradual process of unfolding and developing to flower into our designed function. We go from bud to bloom to flower. And in this culminating process to our life's highest point, we begin to bear the most fruit within our lives and the lives of others. We find ourselves wading into the shallows of *really* living for the first time. And our roots take hold along the refreshing riverbank of purposeful living.

> But blessed is the man who trusts in the Lord, whose confidence is in him. He will be like a tree planted by the water that sends out its roots by the stream. It does not fear when heat comes; its leaves are always green.

It has no worries in a year of drought and never fails
to bear fruit. (Jeremiah 17:7–8 NIV)

For me the distinction between a career and one's mission was
described beautifully by Stephen R. Covey's grandfather.

Life is a mission and not a career, and the purpose
of all our education and knowledge is so that we can
better represent Him and serve that mission of life in
His name and toward His purposes.
—Stephen L. Richards

Yes, certain careers may provide some wonderful things for many
of us. But at the end of the day and at the end of one's life, it will
pale greatly in comparing it to one's mission. For me a *CAREER* is
really all about: Choosing A Revolving Endless Empty Road. It's endless
and empty in that it will never, ever manifest the depth of things
like fulfillment, inner peace, and joyful bliss that carrying out one's
mission will provide.

Everyone has his own specific mission in life; everyone
must carry out a concrete assignment that demands
fulfillment.
—Victor Frankl, *Man's Search for Meaning*

When we truly start living in our sweet spot of Purpose PIE®, we
desire to stay close to God. It is in that tender, intimate closeness that
generates a keen sense of gratitude, as we no longer find ourselves
floating in the sea of inner unfulfillment. We feel whole, healed, and
complete. We feel we are the beloved because we are. And for this,
we are grateful beyond measure. Our labor of love in servanthood

to God and fellow man takes on a different hue because we are now different. This unfolding becomes as natural as the air we breathe. Our daily labor love to God and mankind becomes our personal thank you that can no longer be hidden or hushed. Our coming out party to our responsibility to possibility is starting to flower, and the fragrance is intoxicating.

Along our gratitude discovery trail, I believe the greatest deterrent to experiencing the beauty and fullness of a virtuous life stems from the shackles of guilt. There is no possible way for one to reach the pinnacle of emotional gratitude when one is drowning in a sea of guilt.

> Gratitude is not only the greatest of virtues, but the parent of all the others.
>
> —Marcus Tulluis Cicero

This ongoing guilt-gratitude dilemma is explained beautifully by author Mark Batterson in his book *Wild Goose Chase.*

> Guilt has a shrinking effect. It shrinks our dreams. It shrinks our relationships. It shrinks our hearts. It shrinks our lives to the size of our greatest failures. Grace has the opposite effect. It expands our dreams. It expands our hearts. And it gives us the courage to chase the Wild Goose (Holy Spirit) all the way to the ends of the earth.

Think of it this way:

> Sin – Grace = Guilt
> Sin + Grace = Gratitude

> The grace of God is the difference between drowning in guilt and swimming in gratitude.
>
> -Mark Batterson, author, *Wild Goose Chase*

So where are you in the sea of gratitude? Are you swimming in it? Or are you taking on water like the *Titanic* and drowning in debilitating and toxic guilt? You know it's not easy to forgive yourself for some of life's regrets. But if we are to *really* live and no longer just live, then it is imperative that we do so.

I admit, I struggled with this myself for way too long. Then it hit me one day that if I continued in this fashion, I would be acting with disrespect and a lack of appreciation to the author of forgiveness and grace. Can you imagine how you would feel if you went to great lengths to give a meaningful gift to someone you loved deeply and it was rejected and not received with gratitude?

I'm embarrassed to tell you, but I once made my mom and my wife feel terrible after not receiving their kind and generous gifts with gratitude! In my early teens, my parents gave me a dance birthday party. Right around dusk everyone was slow dancing to a great tune and then my mother came around the corner holding a beautiful candlelit homemade birthday cake. As embarrassed as I was in that moment, I was even more immature and ungracious. As my mother immediately sensed my displeasure, she turned abruptly and made a beeline back into the kitchen. Sensing that I may have messed up in the proper response to gift-giving, I followed my mother into the kitchen. There, I saw her throw (with gusto) my cake into the trash can. Deserved? Absolutely! Did I learn from this gifting experience! I thought I did until ...

Fast forward a couple of decades. I was in my early thirties and had been married to my beautiful wife, Patti, for a few years. It was my birthday, and my wife was so excited as she surprised me with a shiny red Schwinn beach Cruiser bike. Talking about raining on someone's parade. Well I took the cake (no pun intended) that day. Not only did I respond with inappropriate body language, but I asked the thoughtless question, "What am I going to do with a bike?" Because of a racquetball injury a few months earlier, where I dislocated my right knee, my immediate perception was that this gift was untimely. In retrospect it was a perfectly timed gift of love as it would be a great source of physical therapy for me in the healing of my knee. It was a classic case of spouting off before thinking through the moment.

Again, I failed miserably in "receiving gifts graciously 101." And boy did I ever feel guilty for some time after these two experiences. In reflection, because of my youthful immaturity I may not have wanted any birthday cake, but all my friends sure did! As I was demonstrating my emotional lack of appreciation for my bike, I'm sure that if my knee could speak, it would have conveyed its gratitude for the opportunity to heal itself by this gift of love. When you think about God's generous gift of grace for all of us, I see a similar parallel. God's gift of grace is for the taking, all the time. And if and when we choose to receive that glorious gift fully and completely, then we are finally healed from the illness and dis-ease of guilt. Our lives become enriched, and we begin to enrich the lives of others in epic proportion. And as we flower within this spiritual endeavor of magnificence, we are changed forever. Our wellspring of gratitude is now free flowing, and we feel alive as never before.

Accept fully God's generous gift of grace. Then you will be able to experience the fullness of gratitude and the final good-bye to guilt. Then you will be able to keep all the collective junk of life right where it belongs—in the junkyard and not in you!

For those of you who may still be grappling with the heaviness of guilt, then I want you to know that I wrote a song just for you.

I Know Your Name
Lyrics by: Steve Douglas

Had a dream last night, so hard to believe
Yeah, Jesus was givin' a gift to me
We were sittin' at my table, just face-to-face
Felt so unworthy, felt out of place

I was thinkin' ...
I'm a tattered, shattered, worthless fool
I make mistakes and break the rules
I'm damaged goods, with guilt and shame
I can't believe ... He knows my name!

He was holdin' a gift and smilin' at me
Was this a mistake? It had to be!
When I saw my name next to the bow
I said, "Dear, sweet Jesus ... Don't you know?"

I'm a tattered, shattered, worthless fool
I make mistakes and break the rules
I'm damaged goods, with guilt and shame
I can't believe ... You know my name!

Then He reached and handed His gift to me
He said, "You've been blind, but now you'll see."
As I opened my gift and looked inside
My guilt was meltin', to my surprise
As my eyes were readin' His written note
I started believin' the words He wrote.

He said,
"Take my gift ... my gift of grace
So guilt will melt to not a trace
That's why I died, that's why I came
no more guilt, no more shame
because of love, I know your name
because of love ... I know ... your name."

For me, the gift of grace is one of life's great conundrums. How can something so priceless be free? I'm confident that the answer to that thought-provoking question rests in love. Yes, God *really* does know our names because of love, and He wants us to be in a personal, intimate relationship with Him. Guilt and shame are heavy deterrents to the opportunities of intimacy and well-being. Until we learn to open and receive that one-of-a-kind gift in totality, we will never be able to fully experience the sweet emotional stirring that awaits each of us within. So out with guilt and in with gratitude so you can finally get on with God's unique and great commission that He's been patiently waiting to assign you.

The two most important days in life are the day you
are born and the day you discover the reason why.
—Mark Twain, writer

For many years now I have carried with me daily a memento that is my gentle reminder to accept grace fully and to remain ever grateful for this and all my many other blessings. It is my hope that the story I'm about to share with you will make you want to do the same.

On a business trip to Alaska, I was at a conference center in the middle of a break and noticed a colleague of mine was playing with something on the table that I had never seen before. This gentleman happened to be from Columbus, Ohio, and when I asked him what he was playing with, he said it was a buckeye. I had heard of buckeyes, but I guess due to living in Florida all my life, I just had never seen one. After I asked this question, he immediately handed it to me and said, "It's yours, keep it!"

Then I asked him, "What do I do with it?"

He then promptly stated, "I have no earthly idea."

I graciously accepted his gift and thanked him for it. When I flew back to my home in Florida, my buckeye remained on the top of my dresser drawer for months. Then one day I came home from work, and that particular day I was brimming over with gratitude. That's when it hit me! It was around sunset, and the sunlight was entering through our plantation shutters and casting a reflection off the top of the buckeye. This fascinated me, and as I picked it up, a thought came to me. Right then and there I decided I would always carry this with me and i would no longer look at it as my buckeye. From that very moment on, this was going to be my "grateful eye." Whenever I were to see it, touch it, or play with it, it would become my gentle reminder to be grateful for forgiveness, grace, and all the many other blessings I have been gifted with.

So how about you? Is there something you can take with you every day as your gentle reminder to keep swimming in the healing sea of gratitude? If you will do this, what I have found is that on your worst days or your best days, you will remain enveloped in God's generous grace.

> Your worst days are never so bad you are beyond the reach of His grace. And your best days are never so good that you are beyond the need of God's grace. Everyday should be a day of relating to God on the basis of His grace alone.
>
> —Jerry Bridges

So if you haven't yet fully accepted God's generous gift of grace, what are you waiting for? Please don't delay another minute. That beautiful gift is wrapped and has your name on it. Take it! Unwrap it! Embrace it! Own it! Then create your own "grateful eye" to be your gentle reminder to remain daily in a grateful state of mind. For now, your love and your dreams are expanding. No longer laden with the heavy burden of guilt, we now can move forward with the unfolding of our flower within. We now find ourselves standing at the crossroad to our next life. And as we cast our vision down that new path of discovery, we see clearly the raison d'etre of our lives. We realize as never before that our most important reason for existence is all about our most-prized treasure—our relationships.

CHAPTER 6

Raison d'Etre

A friend once told me, "All love has a beginning; only true love has no end." When I reflect on this statement of truth about true love, it fills me with deep and different emotions. In meaningful relationships, we all yearn to be validated and confirmed of our value and significance to others. There is no greater validation of meaningful existence than when we give and receive love. But as with anything else in life, love also comes with inherent risk. There is no greater span of human emotions that one can experience than when one falls in love with another, shares in that love, and then witnesses that love go asunder. Love is a funny thing. In one moment it can come to us when we least expect it and light upon our hearts as naturally and gracefully as a beautiful butterfly may light upon our shoulder. And in another moment it can build a ravaging storm that moves off into the distance we know not where, yet leaves us battered and broken within.

> Tis better to have loved and lost than never to have loved at all.
>
> —Alfred Lord Tennyson

Unlike many things we buy today, love comes with no guarantee. Maybe it works that way because you can't buy love. But then again, we can't buy or earn God's love, yet His love is guaranteed to be everlasting for each and every one of us. Go figure! My takeaway from this is we will never, ever have a greater love than God's everlasting love.

> I have loved you with an everlasting love; I have drawn
> you with loving-kindness. (Jeremiah 31:3 NIV)

Live long enough and we all encounter the full gamut of relational experiences; we gain friendships and we lose friendships. Our friends disappoint us, and yes, we disappoint our friends. Love falls upon us and brings light into our lives. Love falls away from us and darkens our lives with pain. As we ride this rollercoaster of relational ups and downs, we had better have our emotional seat belt ready and secured. And it had better be anchored into where we can measure all other relationships. It must be a fixed center and a rock of unwavering support to where our relational rollercoaster doesn't come tumbling down, and us with it. That fixed center where everything else is supported and can be measured is God. We can be assured that no circumstance, event, or person can ever take away our treasured relationship with God.

> After twenty years of listening to the yearnings of
> people's hearts, I am convinced that human beings
> have an inborn desire for God. Whether we are
> consciously religious or not, this desire is our deepest
> longing and most precious treasure.
> —Dr. Gerald C. May

When earthly love abandons us, many times we may feel that this act is criminal. It's not right, we tell ourselves, and it certainly is not fair. But we need to be extra cautious that we don't become imprisoned in building walls of bitterness, self-pity, and resentment around us. If we are not careful our hurt can easily turn to hate unless we revisit the cross and let it be our gentle reminder of how to take the first step in forgiveness.

When I was a young boy, my mother worked full time and my father worked two jobs for many years of my childhood. Because of this situation, I stayed with my grandparents (my dad's parents) after school and a good part of the summer months. My grandfather died my senior year in high school. As I attended his funeral, it occurred to me that he had never told me that he loved me. In fact, as I reflected further about our relationship, it dawned on me that I didn't have even one kind or loving memory of him. You see, he was chained to the prison of bitterness, and all of his relationships suffered for it. Recently I wrote a song about my grandfather that I would like to share with you.

When Lookin' Back
Lyrics by: Steve Douglas

When lookin' back … The days were long, when I was young
A boy in summer, searchin' for fun
Blue jean shorts, and dirty bare feet
Playin' in the yard and in the street
Had rather been playin' with my granddad
But he didn't like to, he never had
Empty on hugs and I love yous
Missed all my ball games—he had things to do

And that's okay, yeah, that's all right
'Cause maybe in heaven, we'll get it right
See, I'm not here to condemn or judge
And he wasn't here to give or love

When lookin' back ... We never played catch in the yard
He didn't care for games, not even cards
So I threw my ball into the sky
Played solitaire until I cried
The fishin' poles were never used
He always said, "Got things to do."
The years went by, and birthdays too
Never got a card that said, "I love you"

And that's okay, yeah, that's all right
'Cause maybe in heaven, we'll get it right
See, I'm not here to condemn or judge
And he wasn't here to give or love

When lookin' back ... On wasted years
Prayin' for a chance to erase those tears
When lookin' back ... I feel his pain
Sad that drinkin' was his only game

And that's okay, yeah, that's all right
'Cause maybe in heaven we'll get it right
When lookin' back ... On all those days
God, I look to You, and this I pray
I sure hope heaven heals
Yeah, I sure hope heaven heals

Yeah, I said … I sure hope heaven heals
Our pain away … When lookin' back

As a young boy I saw our relationship through my eyes. It was not until many years later that I started to see my grandfather in a different light.

> Don't be fooled into thinking you are alone in your journey. You're not. Your struggle is everyone's struggle. Your pain is everyone's pain. Your power is everyone's power. It is simply that we take different paths along our collective journey.
> —Benjamin Shield, PhD

A piece of Scripture became very freeing for me, and I am certain it can do the same for you, if you trust it.

> Trust in the Lord with all your heart and lean not on your own understanding; in all your ways acknowledge him, and he will make your paths straight. (Proverbs 3:5–6 NIV)

As I began to trust God and no longer leaned on my understanding, I started to see my grandfather in an entirely different light. My grandfather never talked with me about his childhood. In fact, he was pretty much withdrawn about most things in life. But one day I recalled a story that my dad shared with me about my grandfather. It was in that moment that God provided a fresh, new perspective for me. As God moved me with empathy, it started a watershed effect of opening my heart to forgiveness and love for a man that I never really knew. One day my grandfather (seventeen years old) was with his father (a deputy sheriff), and an altercation developed that ended in gunfire. My great-grandfather was shot and killed instantly, and my grandfather was shot just above his heart and nearly died himself. As I started to play out that tragic scene in my mind, I encountered a shift in perception.

In 1921 my great-grandfather was the first Palm Beach County deputy sheriff who was killed in the line of duty. Not only did my grandfather witness that horrific event in seeing his father murdered, but he also physically suffered as he was seriously injured. It suddenly became very clear to me how easy it would be to become shackled to the prison of bitterness. From this I started to take my eyes off of myself. I began to see and feel how my grandfather as a young boy must have been totally devastated by this personal tragedy. My grandfather became an alcoholic and heavy chain smoker, which led to throat cancer and ultimately to his demise. But in my opinion, my grandfather died long before his physical death. His disease of bitterness killed all of his relationships. He lived a lonely life and died a lonely man, and all of the relationships around him suffered for it.

> I have absolutely no pleasure in the stimulants in which I sometimes so madly indulge. It has not been in the pursuit of pleasure that I have periled life and reputation and reason. It has been the desperate attempt to escape from torturing memories, from sense of insupportable loneliness and a dread of some strange impending doom.
>
> —Edgar Allan Poe

Relationships are our most prized treasure. Relationships are the most important reason for our existence. When we're *in* relationship, we find ourselves *in* an opportunity for a cornucopia of rich meaning and significance. When we're *out* of relationship, we find ourselves *out* standing in an emotional soup line called loneliness, the worst kind of poverty.

> The most terrible poverty is loneliness, and the feeling of being unloved.
>
> —Mother Teresa

Late one afternoon in my office, my mother and I were having a conversation over the phone. Before our call ended, she shared with me a story about one of her friends. My mom and this friend of hers used to play tennis together and then go have lunch. One day her friend was describing an intimate part of her life. She was telling my mother that for so many years she was all by herself and was so lonely. She wanted so much to be in a loving relationship with someone. Then one day, lo and behold, Mr. Right showed up. They dated, fell in love, got married, were happily married, started having problems, and ultimately got divorced. Through all the years of emotional swirl, she shared a thought-provoking message with my mom. She said in reflecting on her life, she realized she was far lonelier in the years when she was in love and things weren't right than all the years she was all by herself and yearning for love. As we ended our conversation, I reached for a pen and piece of paper and wrote the words of "Lonely in Two." The next day when I came into my office I spotted my scribbled note, and as I reflected on my mom's earlier story, I wrote a song about loneliness in relationships. Here is my song.

Lonely in Two
Lyrics by: Steve Douglas

Been by myself for days on end
Just me and lonely, my only friend
Thought that was rough, yeah ... little did I know
There's a much tougher place where you can go
So much more than twice the pain
When two in love are lonely and lose their way

It's a sadder sad and a bluer blue
The pain cuts deeper, yeah ... deeper in you
When that lonely bug bites and leaves its sting
Yeah, lonely in two, it's a tragic thing

The love's still there, but the magic dies
Both lost for words, with no reason why
Shoulder to shoulder, and hearts just driftin', yeah ... driftin' apart

Prayin' for a miracle, for a fresh new start
No mistakin' that fire that used to be
Now a chill fills their rooms with complacency

It's a sadder sad and a bluer blue
The pain cuts deeper, yeah ... deeper in you
When that lonely bug bites and leaves its sting
Yeah, lonely in two, it's a tragic thing

Both waitin' for the other to get things right
And time's just movin' by, no healin' in sight
The wrinkles are a showin', and shades of gray movin' in

But the hole in their hearts, it's their greatest sin
It's a sadder sad and a bluer blue
When the one you love turns their back on you

Some say God made man 'cause He got lonely
I say that may be true and maybe not
But I sure know what God would love to stop
When you turn your back and treat Him coldly
Yeah, that even wounds the One and Only
It's the saddest sad and the bluest blue
No deeper pain will cut in you
Than the sting, that tragic thing ... of ... lonely in two

Yeah, "Lonely In Two." A bitter sting and a tragic thing. The hole in their hearts, it's their greatest sin. The sin of broken promises of two in love. The letdown and disappointment of commitment and expectations that fall short from the ones we love in our cherished relationships can many times leave us with a gaping hole in our hearts. They say time is a great healer. I say God is the greatest healer. And when we have a "Lonely In Two" going on in our personal, family, or marital relationships, we had better take our hurtful lonely to the One and Only. After all, He is our greatest source for hope of ever healing.

Personally, I don't believe God made man because he was lonely. God certainly didn't need to create the universe, but He obviously chose to. And because God is love and love is best expressed and experienced within relationships, God chose to create life and people as an intimate expression of His perfect love. God even admits that He's a jealous God. So when we turn our backs and treat Him coldly, yeah ... that even wounds the One and Only. Every time we withdraw and turn away from God who is perfect love, we start to lose our way.

That's why it's so vital to have a daily communion and quiet time with God. For me, the early morning works best. It affords me the opportunity to become still and quiet and to rediscover all over again the enormity of God's generous and perfect love. I start to understand and to feel deeply that God truly wants what's best for me. I love to check in with Him daily to stay in the sweet spot of His love and His specifically designed mission for me. I certainly don't want to turn my back to Him and manifest a "Lonely in Two" relationship. It is in this daily sacred encounter that gives me the courage and the strength to take on a servant's heart for God and humanity. As our relationship becomes more personal and intimate in nature, I start to see more clearly that we all have been assigned a unique, one-of-a-kind sweet-spot mission in this life. From this I have discovered that there is one common thread interconnecting all of our collective lives. That common thread is love.

> For the first time in my life I saw the truth ... that love is the ultimate and highest goal to which man can aspire. Then I grasped the meaning of the greatest secret that human poetry and human thought and belief have to impart: The salvation of man is through love and in love. I understand how a man who has nothing left in the world may still know bliss.
> —Victor Frankl, *Man's Search for Meaning.*

Even though Victor Frankl endured three years of extreme suffering in the Nazi concentration camp at Auschwitz and had everything of importance stripped from him, he realized more than ever that the most noble and sacred goal that we all should aspire to is love. There is no greater investment that any of us can make than the love of investing in relational capital. The greatest return on investment (ROI) that we could ever hope to have will always come from investing in people and relationships, especially when it is done in the spirit of love.

> Treasure your relationships; they are worth more than your possessions.
>
> —Anthony J. D'Angelo

Recently I lost two of my best friends within six months of each other. One was from complications of what was hoped to be a routine heart procedure. The other was from what started as a small mole on his back that later turned into melanoma. I was nothing short of devastated! Luckily a friend of mine gave me a book at that time, and it was truly divine intervention. The book was Philip Yancey's *Where Is God When You Hurt.*

This read is filled with many valuable insights and nuggets of wisdom. But there was one thing that I garnered from this book that rescued me from the emotional cesspool that I was drowning in. And here it is: No matter the adversity, setback, or wounding that has fallen upon us, we can still choose to love and trust God in spite of it. As I chose to do just that, it has made all the difference in the world. Do I still miss my friends and deeply long for that special bond we had for decades? You bet I do! But I found that when I chose to trust and love God through *all* my trials, then I experienced the fullness of His loving grace.

When we still trust and love Him in spite of all our brokenness, we will find that His grace is always bigger than our pain. We become like the prodigal son returning home to the loving arms of his father. We no longer accept the rejection of the world that imprisons us but accept the freedom to be the children of God that we are. We learn that our pain only intensifies when we run away from the place where God dwells. If we run away, it becomes more difficult for us to hear the sweet, tender voice that calls us the beloved. The world's love is and will always be conditional. God's love is far more generous and tenderhearted that that, as His arms are always opened wide for our return.

Yes, God sees our mistakes and mess ups and how we are marred beyond measure. But He also sees us through the eyes of a loving Father, and in that vision He also sees our value. Once we start to understand the depth of His grace, comprised of compassion, forgiveness, and unconditional love in spite of all our defects, then we become less encumbered to offer the same gift to others. And here's the deal: live long enough and we all find out that life *ain't* for sissies! Eventually we begin to see that no friendship, marriage, or person is perfect. All of it is flawed in one way or another. But when we let love become the emotional superglue in the cracks of our relationships, we find ourselves becoming more tolerant and compassionate. Our heavy yoke of strife that has burdened our relationships becomes lighter, and we become more desirous to love and serve God and others, in spite of all of our angst.

For any of you that may struggle with tolerance and compassion, I highly recommend the movie *The Doctor. The Doctor,* starring William Hurt, is based on a true story about a brilliant heart surgeon who lacks sensitivity and emotional connection with his patients. All of this cold detachment comes to a screeching halt when he is diagnosed with throat cancer, and he finds himself in the care of a physician much like himself. Guess what? He doesn't like it one bit. Then all of a sudden the light bulb comes on, and he now understands a core truth among human beings. No one really cares about how much you know until they first know how much you care. This is what the Purpose PIE® journey is all about—caring for God, caring for others, and yes, even caring for ourselves. And how we nurture this care or not is a daily battleground that I call the everyday encounter.

CHAPTER 7

Everyday Encounter

Each and every day we all face an everyday encounter—an encounter of two voices and two choices. One voice chatters and one voice matters. One voice debilitates and one voice liberates. One voice whispers doubts to smolder dreams, and one voice whispers dares to shoulder dreams.

> Our doubts are traitors, and make us lose the good we
> oft might win by fearing the attempt.
> —William Shakespeare

Most of us don't even have a clue about this daily mental and emotional battleground that is constantly raging within our minds. I admit it. For years I was totally oblivious to it. Thank God this is no longer the case. This understanding is the reason you are now holding my book in your hands. Now I want to share with you so you also may move forward with your life mission and find yourself basking in the sweet spot of purposeful living.

My wife and I love the TV show *The Voice*. For those of you not familiar with the program, it provides talented singers an opportunity to demonstrate their gifted voices to four coaches (singing professionals). At the onset the coaches do not see what they look like as they are only allowed to hear the voice. As long as one or more of the coaches select a contestant to advance in the contest on their team, then they will move forward in the competition to what is called the battle rounds. For each battle round one voice is selected as a winning voice. The voice not selected is out of the competition and heads home, unless one or more of the coaches hits the "red steal button." When this happens, the coach or coaches are saying they deem the talent of the contestant worthy enough for another battle round.

Every day we have battle rounds with two voices. Every day we choose one voice over the other. When things don't appear to be going well for us and we sense we need someone to still believe in us and give us another chance, oftentimes we don't recognize that the answer to our burning wish is much closer than we realize. All we really need is a bit more sensitivity and a bit more awareness to the great truth that lies within each and every one of us.

> And I will ask the Father, and he will give you another Counselor to be with you forever—the Spirit of truth. The world cannot accept him, because it neither sees him nor knows him. But you know him, for he lives with you and will be in you. (John 14:16–17 NIV)

We all have the perfect voice within. We all have the voice of truth just waiting to coach us up to greatness. There's just one variation between the show and our personal lives. A coach doesn't choose us; we choose the coach. See, our God is a God who has blessed us with choice. We could never make a better choice than to choose God to be the one that coaches us through the battle rounds of life. All we have to do is come near to Him and stay near to Him and the rest will fall into place, in that we will now be in the right place.

> Come near *to* God and he will come near *to* you. (James 4:8 NIV)

I find it fascinating how such a small word can take on such ginormous depth and meaning. For example, take the word *to* in the James 4:8 verse. According to *the American Heritage Dictionary*, the definition of *to* is, "In a direction toward reaching as far as in contact with; cheek to cheek in front of: face to face, in relation with; parallel to the road." Wow! What a thought. Just knowing that when we come near *to* God, He comes near *to* us—cheek to cheek, face-to-face, and in relation with. Yeah, "spiritually partnering in relational intimacy together." Want the best coach, partner, or friend you could possibly have? Then come near *to* God and He will come near *to* you! He's waiting for you to coach you up so that you may deliver your one-of-a-kind song to the world and leave it in a better place than you found it. So are you looking for someone to believe in you and give you another chance? Looking for new, fresh hope and a future that will be difficult to take all in? Then look no further. Your perfect voice lies within and is waiting to co-create with you and to play out the perfect plan to not harm you but prosper you.

> "For I know the plans I have for you," declares the Lord, "plans to prosper you and not to harm you, plans to give you hope and a future." (Jeremiah 29:11 NIV)

Hope is a funny thing in how it works with our minds and plays on our emotions. As long as we have hope, we can lose multiple battle rounds in life and still proceed with moxie to endure. We can still attempt to forge through our difficulties. It's where we lose our hope that life becomes so painful that we find ourselves making camp on the battlefield of meaninglessness. Here we've not just lost in the battle rounds; we lost the war. If you even remotely feel like this, I'm here to tell you that that's a lie. There's something that lies in you that is so great and is just waiting for you *to* make the move *to* another chance, *to* hope, and *to* a future of prosperity and greatness that has been personally designed for you before you took your first breath. All you have *to* do is believe and make that first step *to* God. What you will discover is that this Friend will be there waiting for you to start an intimate and connecting friendship like you've never seen.

> God doth not ride me as a horse and guide me I know
> not whither myself; but converseth with me in such
> a dialect as I understand fully and can make others
> understand.
>
> —Henry More, 1614–1687

Two voices. Two choices. From the beginning of time with Adam and Eve in the garden of Eden to present day, we've been in a constant battleground of two clear and distinct voices. I can just imagine how Adam's two voices may have been doing battle with each other as he was being tempted in the garden.

"Ah, to choose to eat from so many beautiful trees in the garden."

"But I must not eat from the Tree of Knowledge of Good and Evil, or surely I will die."

"Ah, but that one tree is so pleasing to the eye."

"No, I better not do it."

"But wouldn't it also be desirable for gaining wisdom?"

"I'm curious about gaining wisdom, but I better not do it."

"Are you sure about that?"

"I don't know."

"Ah, just take one bite."

"I don't think so."

"One bite won't hurt anything."

"Are you sure?"

"Look how delicious and pleasing it looks."

"Ah, okay. I guess a bite or two won't hurt anything ..." (*Crunch!*)

It seems as if in everything in life, there is a polar opposite that goes hand in hand. There's a constant tug-of-war in our daily thoughts, choices, and decisions. So many things we are aware of and unaware of come into play in keeping us tethered to the pole of sabotage and self-sabotage. Unawareness, bad choices, and lame excuses encumber us from venturing into the land of exuberant efflorescence. These things hold us hostage from experiencing the enthusiastic wonder of watching firsthand our lives unfold and develop into a state of flower. We should be culminating into our highest point and building into a deafening crescendo of magnificence. Instead, we're still wandering aimlessly in the valley of quiet desperation, asking ourselves, "What happened?"

> The things we cherish most are at the mercy of the things we cherish least.
>
> —William James, 1842–1910

Not living in the white-hot center of a passionate, mission-inspired life comes at the expense of ego, fear, procrastination, rejection, criticism, rationalization, and anything else you may feel compelled to add to the list that keeps us throttled in the mediocre gear of neutral.

> If you want to identify me, ask me not where I live or what I like to eat or how I comb my hair, but ask me

what I am living for, in detail. Ask me what I think is keeping me from living fully for the thing I want to live for.

—Thomas Merton, author

So many today think that the only nemesis to living a life of greatness is due to the worldly *sabotage* of people and circumstances. Yes, rejection and criticism hurt, and it's disappointing when life kicks you in the fanny with some harsh surprise. But the way I see it, the people who struggle the greatest in this area are the ones who give way too much credence to the opinions of others. And this toxic poison becomes even more impactful when God is not an integral facet within their lives. For me, I view this form of SABO^3TAGE as: Self-Absorbed Battleground Of Others Opinions That's Always God Excluded.

There is no doubt that sabotage can come in all varieties from others and the ever-revolving twists and turns of life's unexpected circumstances. But let me let you in on a truism that far too many people suffer with repeatedly on an ongoing, day-to-day basis and are not even remotely aware of this invisible, life-sucking, debilitating force that takes great pleasure in cutting the very heart right out of one ever fulfilling the embodiment of their hopes, dreams, and destiny. It's called self-sabotage, and nothing is more lethal in preventing one from living a fruitful and purposeful life. *SELF* in this context stands for: Selecting EGO-Led Fear.

We put far too much value in worldly things, especially the O^3, opinions of others. Let me let you in on a little secret that will help you with the opinion of others battle each and every time: once you discover and start living in the sweet-spot mission of your life, you will be co-creating with *God*. You will be the conduit, the vessel, and the clay that is being shaped by the Purpose PIE® Potter! So whether you attain kudos or condemnation (trust me, you'll get both) on your art, creativity, contribution, etc., this is the emotional mind-set I suggest you own going forward.

Every time you receive a compliment or high mark for your sweet-spot endeavors, *do not* take the credit. Be appreciative and grateful, but give the credit where the credit is due: to *God*.

> I am the Lord; that is my name! I will not give my glory
> to another or my praise to idols. (Isaiah 42:8 NIV)

Here's the part that drops an emotional A-bomb right on the negative, cynical, and condemning opinions of others and blows it away as easy as saying, "One, two, three." Every time you encounter negativity in any fashion in regard to your God-ordained mission, think or say this: "Since I can't take the credit, don't blame me, 'cause now you know it's not my fault." This will take the sting out of their stinger every time. Guess what? God is a lot tougher and far more resilient than we could ever be. After all, hasn't God been taking heaps of rejection from the very beginning of humanity to the present day? He still forgives us totally and even knows our names, all because of love. We serve an amazing God! So the next time someone poo-poos your Purpose PIE®, don't let the opinions of others cause your dreams to die.

Two voices. Two choices. One debilitates. One liberates. One from darkness. One from light. How we go about following one or the other makes all the difference in just living or *really* living. The choice is ours, and whether we believe it or not, we make it every day. We either tumble in the dark abyss or we tread on pearly heights. Most of us have two distinct lives: the one we are living and the unlived life within.

> It's never too late to be who you might have been.
> —George Eliot (1819–1880), writer

One voice is as happy as a clam with just the way things are. The other voice is patiently waiting with its emotional hand out for you to take it and begin your journey to greatness. Since I've been aware of the two voices, I've seen several names for the one that breeds deception and is *not* our friend. Freud called it the "death wish." Steven Pressfield, author of *The War of Art,* calls it "resistance." Julia Cameron, author of *The Artist's Way,* calls it the "the censor," a nasty internal and external critic. I make reference to it as our Purpose PIE® Perpetrator. Why perpetrator? Because a perpetrator is described as one who brings about deception or a crime. And what this master of deceit has manifested since the beginning of time is beyond criminal. This voice has participated in sending millions upon millions of people to their graves with their one-of-a-kind song of life still in them.

> While we have the gift of life, it seems to me the only
> tragedy is to allow part of us to die ... whether it is our
> spirit, our creativity, or our glorious uniqueness.
> —Gilda Radner, comedian (1946–1989)

If there is anyone or anything that should be sentenced to prison, it would be the Perpetrator—the one who cunningly deceives us and thwarts us from delivering God's divine calling. Going forward I would like to share with you how you can at least keep him at bay, if not locked up and imprisoned. The antithesis of the Perpetrator is the Purpose PIE® Pilgrim. Why the term *pilgrim*? Because a pilgrim is someone who travels to a holy place, one who journeys to foreign lands, and one who is a traveling devotee. Yes, your Purpose PIE® Pilgrim is a devotee to you. He is an ardent and enthusiastic supporter, advocate, and admirer of you. He's a huge fan of yours! He is waiting to take you on a spectacular and priceless pilgrimage. But first you come to Him and then He will come to you. You first must knock and then He will open the door to you. Soon you will start to receive numinous nutrition and some Godwinks along the way. Your Purpose PIE® Pilgrim is your voice of truth. It is your Counselor in a holy encounter that will guide you to holy ground.

For nearly fifteen years I have had a keen fascination and a feeling of adornment for the whole Purpose PIE® concept. I always felt I would eventually get around to further exploring and eventually completing it. I just didn't know when. Then one day I was talking with a friend of mine over the phone. We had not talked in some time, and we were catching up with the normal chit-chat. I was sharing with him that I still had my finger in Purpose PIE®, so to speak. Then a comment was made, and all of a sudden it felt as if someone had thrown a pie in my face and I was choking down some humble pie, whether I wanted to or not.

Don't get me wrong. His comment was not mean spirited in any way, shape, or form. But it was brutally honest, and that raw honesty didn't beat around the bush but went straight to the heart of the matter. It occurred to me in that very moment of how cheap talk is. I'd been yammering for years upon years about this so-called grand vision of Purpose PIE® that I had. Then out of nowhere my hand was called and what I had to show wasn't pretty. For years I had been talkin' the talk and not walkin' the walk.

It reminded me of a saying that my father said to me when I would fall short of a desired outcome. "You're gonna do wonders but eat rotten cucumbers." And when my friend said so candidly, "Goodness, Steve, you've been talking about that for years now," it felt as if I had landed in a dumpster of rotten, stinking cucumbers. His intention was not to criticize, but it sure had a resounding, truthful ring to it.

At that time I didn't have the keen understanding of how cunning the voice of the Perpetrator can be. I certainly do now, and that's why Purpose PIE® is no longer a dream but a reality! I'm sharing this with you because I'm confident that your Perpetrator is doing the exact same thing to you. It's time to stop that crazy noise that will lead you to nowhere land.

The way I now look at this Perpetrator-Pilgrim thing is that it reminds me a lot about electricity. Just like I don't understand all there is to know about electricity, there is one thing I truly know about it. It can bring beautiful light to you and provide many daily comforts in serving you well. If you're not careful, it can also injure you and even kill you. These two voices act in the same capacity. The voice of your Pilgrim can bring you in the light and brighten your life in ways you never could imagine. The voice of your Perpetrator can dilute, diminish, and yes, even destroy your hopes and dreams and rightful destiny. When you're not totally aware of this everyday encounter, it can bring about a slow, inner death that you will be completely oblivious to.

> There is a second self inside you—an inner, shadow self. This self doesn't care about you. It doesn't love you. It has its own agenda, and it will kill you. It will kill you like cancer. It will kill you to achieve its agenda, which is to prevent you from actualizing your self from becoming who you really are.
>
> —Rabbi Mordecai Finley, from *Turning Pro*,
> by Steven Pressfield

Let's say you're a frog and you come across this beautiful pond. You jump in and it feels like frog heaven. But what you're not aware of is that you have a perpetrator lurking, and this perpetrator happens to love frog legs! And your adversary has created a pond where he can raise the temperature by one degree every few hours. Guess what? As you're frolicking in the lily pond, you are not even remotely aware of the slow and gradual change of temperature. You lose track of time. Not only that, but you lose your life because you now find yourself swimming around in a 212-degree environment. When that happens, you can say the frog legs are cooked, and dreams right along with them. Part of my mission is to keep you away from the 212-degree environment. To give you some added clarity about this two-voice dynamic, I've created this diagram for you.

Purpose PIE® Perpetrator	Purpose PIE® Pilgrim
Ego	Spirit
Fear	Love
Deception	Truth
Hinder	Help
Sabotage	Empower
Job	Dream
Plaintive	Purposeful
Career	Calling
Status Quo	Mission
Crumbs	PIE

The Perpetrator operates of this world. The Pilgrim helps us prepare for the next. The worldly voice is fed by fear—our fear; otherwise it would die. Our heavenly voice is our spiritual guide to truth and total fulfillment, all in the name of love. Our dark voice deceives, hinders, and sabotages us in remaining in the mundane of the status quo. Our voice of light enlightens and empowers us and leads us on a spiritual pilgrimage to the likes of which we've never seen. The perpetrator builds walls in the name of scarcity and safety in protecting me, myself, and I. The Pilgrim breaks down walls in the spirit of abundance and exploration into the brave new world of servanthood and contribution.

The Perpetrator barely sustains you with crumbs of life that are filled with lies. It tells you daily in its subtle, crafty way to not push the envelope of life. You're not good enough to attempt to extend your current limits of performance. You've really not innovative, imaginative, or creative enough to go beyond commonly accepted boundaries. You're fine just the way you are, wallowing in mediocrity and groveling for crumbs in your safe haven of just living. The Pilgrim whispers soft and tender words of loving truth. "Your life *really* can be different. In fact, I've prepared a table for you to feast upon. A smorgasbord of the sweetest sweets in all of life. A unique and one-of-a-kind Purpose PIE® of Passion, Inspiration, and Enthusiasm is yours for the asking."

Ready to taste and experience your first slice? Then let's get down to work together in making it a reality. In fact, this is our first line of defense against the Perpetrator. We work together. We spiritually partner in relational intimacy together.

> Inspiration exists, but it has to find you working.
> —Pablo Picasso, painter

> And we know that in all things God works for the good of those who love him, who have been called according to his purpose. (Romans 8:28 NIV)

Oh, how comforting to know that God is our wonderful partner in our labor (of love) and because of this, all things work together and we are fitting into a plan for good.

> We come into this world with a specific, personal destiny. We have a job to do, a calling to enact, a self to become. We are who we are from the cradle, and we're

stuck with it. Our job in this lifetime is not to shape ourselves into some ideal image we ought to be, but to find out who we already are and become it.

—Steven Pressfield, *The War of Art*

The way I see it, there's no getting around it. If we want to participate in creating anything of meaning and significance then we have to go to work. We have to show up and get 'er done. Think about it. When God decided to create the universe, before He took that well-deserved seventh day of rest, He had to first work and labor with His creativity. Remember the saying, "Are you talking the talk or walking the walk?" God always walks the walk. So many times our talk stymies us from walking on our designed path in completing and fulfilling our destiny.

If you want a place in the sun, you've got to put up with a few blisters.

—Abigail Van Buren, columnist

Nobody ever drowned in his own sweat.

—Ann Landers, advice columnist

And the more we *talk* about our dreams, the more fuel to the fire we give to the Perpetrator in increasing the decibel of the daily blah-blah-blahs. We've all had the blahs before and know how rotten that feeling is. It's no wonder because blah is a word commonly used to describe an emotional state in which the person feels a sense of having no hope, usually a deep depression.

Trust me, I know. I talked a great game about my vision of Purpose PIE® for years on end. I didn't even have a clue that my designed destiny was slowly but surely dying—that's until I became intentional to work my mission. From here a fascinating thing happened. As I began to work my mission with a labor of love, I noticed that I started receiving an inordinate amount of help. Thoughts, ideas, people, and unexpected opportunities would show up out of the blue. Synchronistic events would present themselves over and over again. Each time they did, I found myself shaking my head, pinching myself, and whispering the word *goosies*, over and over again.

I also noticed that the intensity of the voice coming out of the pie-hole of the Perpetrator was subsiding. This made a lot of sense, as I was no longer feeding it the fear I had been for years. It was loosening its grip on me and becoming weaker as God gave me renewed and added strength daily.

As I moved forward on my Purpose PIE® path, I began to notice some unexpected but very welcomed and pleasant changes taking place. I started becoming more hopeful and expectant than ever before. My confidence started to shoot through the roof because I knew beyond a shadow of a doubt that the *help* that was now my daily companion was perfect and invincible in every way imaginable. And because of this truth, I found myself with a building sensation of fulfillment, inner peace, and gratitude that was beyond description. I also had a feeling of being loved so deeply that many times it would catch me unexpectedly, and out of nowhere I would find myself welling up with blissful tears. From this experience I became aware that my love for God, others, and even myself was changing to a more tender and caring love. But of all these wonderful changes that were unfolding before me, the most impactful change was that I felt *alive* as never before! I am here to tell you that if you find yourself not white hot, on fire *alive* then you can no longer afford not to take the risk to get you there.

There is the risk you cannot afford to take, there is the risk you cannot afford not to take.

—Peter Drucker

So where are you in your personal challenge and response to the opinions of others? How have you been stacking up against the dream-sucking chatter of your perpetrator? Which voice are you adhering to in being your compass into the future?

The only way to be truly satisfied is to do what you believe is great work. And the only way to do great work is to love what you do.

—Steve Jobs, cofounder, Apple

So why expend any more energy into anything that is secondary in your life? Why not be all in to what really matters the most? Isn't it about time to cease and desist the crawling around for life's CRUMBS: Choosing Regretful, Unfulfilling Mistakes But Safe.

Why not trying to replace being safe with being courageous in pulling yourself out of the messy quagmire of complacency? Trust me on this—there is no greater labor of love than when you playfully work in co-creating with God. It is here where you witness firsthand how God is changing you within. The transformation from this holy encounter is where daring dreams begin to unfold. Once you find your true sacred voice, you know you can venture into the sweet spot of greatness as you inspire others of find theirs.

Deep within each one of us there is an inner longing to live a life of *greatness* and contribution – to really matter, to really make a difference. We may doubt ourselves and our ability to do so, but I want you to know of my deep conviction that *you can* live such a life. You have the potential in you. We all do. It is the birthright of the human family.

—Steven Covey, author,
The Eighth Habit from Effectiveness to Greatness

So are you with me, ready to create and capture some daring dreams to greatness? I sure am! Now that you're fully aware about our everyday encounter, let's counter with taking our daring dreams:

- to our voice that really cares and matters;
- to our voice that can make our impossible His possible; and
- to our voice that knows our name, all because of love.

CHAPTER 8

Daring Dreams

You see things; and you say, "Why?" But I dream things
that never were; and I say, "Why not?"
                                    —George Bernard Shaw, writer

We all have dreams when we are sleeping. But the dreams I wish to share with you are about daring dreams when we are wide awake where we allow our imaginations to soar and do our part in willing the impossible to transform itself to the possible. The way I see it, the *IM* in impossible should stand for *I Manifest* possible. We initiate the process of manifesting the spiritual partnering. We give ourselves the green light in having bold, audacious, and venturesome dreams of what could be. We step into this realm of faith because we choose to believe in the obvious, apparent, and unmistakable—the truth that with God all things are possible.

Those who dream by day are cognizant of many things
that escape those who dream only at night.
                                    —Edgar Allan Poe, poet

The way I see it is that we first must believe for God to achieve. It's certainly not the case of *can* He make the impossible possible. It's the fact of whether He's *willing* to or not. I find the story about Jesus and the leper in the book of Matthew fascinating. When the leper came and knelt before Jesus, he said, "Lord, if You are *willing*, You can make me clean." And Jesus responded by reaching out His hand and touched the leper as He said, "I am willing. Be clean!" The leper not for one second doubted if Christ could heal him. He believed he would be healed if Christ was *willing*. When God becomes willing to answer a daring dream of ours, I see WILLING as: When Imagination Lets Loose Impossible Near God.

This is when we no longer are entrenched and embedded in the impossible. We can let loose of the impossible and now be expectant and openhearted to what could be. By faith, our imagination soars into daring dreams as we believe God truly can turn impossible to possible if He's willing.

> I have learned to use the word "impossible" with the greatest caution.
>
> —Wernher von Braun, rocket engineer

I'm sure Walt Disney would have told you that there is no greater imagination than that of a child. And when you think about it, it makes a lot of sense. They just haven't yet received the constant barrage of nos. No, that can't be done. No, that's impossible. No, that will never happen in a million years, etc. But many children become living examples of the truth found in Matthew 19:26 when Jesus says, "With man this is impossible, but with God all things are possible."

I'd like to share with you where I let my imagination *soar* as a child and believed wholeheartedly that God would turn my dream of what the world said was impossible into the possibility of wonder and awe.

After my parents fell in love and got married, the dream of having a large family came crashing down when I was born. I was born ten and a half months after my parents were married and I almost killed my mother (not intentionally of course) when she delivered me. Five days after I was born, my mother and I came home in an ambulance. Because of complications my mom experienced in labor, her doctor informed her that it would be *impossible* for her to ever have children again. From the earliest time I can remember, I always had the dream of having a brother. I knew exactly what I wanted—not a sister or sisters and not even brothers, but *a* brother. In fact, I wanted and dreamt of having a brother so intently that I created an imaginary character in my mind. He even had a name. His name was Cotty. This Cotty guy at first caused some cautious concern for my parents, but they later became okay with my imaginary brother.

> When you have a dream, you've got to grab it and never let go.
> —Carol Burnett, comedian

There were times when my mother would ask me if Cotty would like to have dinner with us, and after my enthusiastic *yes*, she would graciously set another table setting. Now that's the team spirit for expanding one's imagination! But of all the intimate memories that I reflect on when I think of Cotty, the most endearing were the times when I prayed right before going to bed. I had no earthly idea how Cotty was going to ultimately show up, but I knew he was coming. I believed with all my heart that God knew my deepest desire and dream and would ultimately bless me with the experience of having a brother. I was confident that God would deliver.

The years rolled by, the prayers continued, and I now was a senior in high school. Then one day out of the blue, my mom knocked on my bedroom door. She came in, grabbed my hand as we sat on my bed, and told me she was going to the doctor that day. She encouraged me not to get too excited, but there was a chance we would be adding a new family member. I cannot even remotely describe to you the exhilaration I had at that incredible moment of time. There was absolutely *no way* I could wait to get home from school to hear the news. Those were the days when there was no such thing as a cell phone. So my mother and I agreed that I would call her at a certain time and she would share the news with me at that time.

After getting permission from my teacher, I went to the guidance counselor's office to make the call. I can remember vividly as I was dialing that old rotary style phone, my hands were trembling like never before. As the phone rang, my heart was pounding, and then my mother finally picked up the phone. Silence over the phone ... and then I heard those magical, dreamlike words: "I'm pregnant!" I immediately screamed into the phone, "I love you," slammed down the phone, and went running down the corridor of classrooms with arms raised high, yelling at the top of my lungs, *"My mother's pregnant! My mother's pregnant!"*

Then the wait began—the anticipation of boy or girl. At that time the medical community didn't have the capability to determine the sex. You had to wait and wait for nine *long* months. For me it was an eternity, but I had a strong sensation that my brother I had been dreaming about for years was getting ready for his grand entry into the world. On December 2, 1969, my mother gave birth to a beautiful, healthy son.

> People who say it cannot be done should not interrupt
> those who are doing it.
> —George Bernard Shaw, writer

Can you believe it? For eighteen and a half years I had been dreaming and praying for Cotty, but my parents named my brother Joey Michael. But you know what? I could not have cared less. They could have named him *Bozo* or anything else. *Any* name was perfectly fine with me. It really didn't matter, because when I held my brother in my arms minutes after he was born, with tears running down my face, I knew right then and there that I was witnessing a miracle of miracles. My mother didn't just deliver a child into the world, but God delivered on the impossible. Yeah, God opened a door I had been knocking on forever. He said yes to possible when the world said impossible. He showed through His love and grace that daring dreams really can come true. When it did, it changed my life forever!

So where are you in the department of daring dreams? What daring dream is tugging at your heart but so far the world has poo-poood it into the trash heap of impossible? Going forward I want you to have this kind of mind-set. When you experience your everyday encounter with the master of sabotage (the Perpetrator), I want you to be *daring*! To become *DARING* is all about: Dreaming Above Reality Inspired Near God.

I certainly understand it's not easy to dream above and beyond what's not yet real, but when you stay near God and remain totally committed to His inspirational guidance, then you will know the way. When you become relentless and committed to holding onto your daring dream as a pit bull would hang on to a sixteen-ounce New York strip, then you eventually will witness a power unleash itself within.

> Never underestimate the power of dreams and the influence of the human spirit. We are all the same in this notion: The potential for greatness lives within each of us.
>
> —Wilma Rudolf

When I make reference to being committed, I'm not speaking about being involved; I'm talking about *total* commitment. This reminds me of the story about the chicken and the pig that were asked if they would make a contribution to breakfast. The chicken agreed to furnish the eggs. Now that's being involved. The pig, on the other hand, agreed to furnish the bacon. Now that's *total* commitment!

> Until one is committed, there is hesitancy, the chance to draw back, always ineffectiveness concerning all acts of initiative and creation. There is one elementary truth, the ignorance of which kills countless ideas and splendid plans: that the moment one definitely commits oneself, then Providence moves too. All sorts of things occur to help one that would never otherwise have occurred. A whole stream of events issues from the decision raising in one's favor all manner of events, meetings and material assistance which no one could have dreamed would have come their way.
>
> —W. H. Murray

Yeah, *total* commitment. Being all in! No wavering or waffling to the vision of your mission coming true. Many times when we commit then God permits or makes possible.

Today many people wear protective goggles in different aspects of work and play to safeguard their vision and to be able to complete whatever task is at hand. Goggles come in many different colors, sizes, and shapes that we can select from. Used as a metaphor, I see many similar options to choose from as we select our protective eyewear to aid in the attainment of our vision's mission.

When it comes to selecting your unique and personal goggles in protecting your vision to your mission, I want you to be keenly aware of something on a day-to-day basis. I want you to see through your *GOGGLES* in this light: Good Or Great, God Lets Everyone Select.

Yes, God allows everyone to choose or select a life of greatness or not. So I implore to you, don't allow the good things to thwart the great things that are patiently waiting to present themselves to you. There are a kazillion good things, programs, and events that we can participate in that will have limited to no added value in advocating our God-sized dreams. We have to learn to say no to good and be all in, committed to saying yes to great things. Our greatness lies within discovering and then playing/working out our designed destiny.

> What you do makes a difference, and you have to decide what kind of difference you want to make.
>
> —Jane Godall

> To know what you prefer instead of humbly saying amen to what the world tells you you ought to prefer, is to have kept your soul alive.
>
> —Robert Louis Stevenson

I want to revisit this choice thing with you again. You see, as great and loving as God is, He is not going to ram anything down our gullet. He allows us the privilege and blessing of choice. It is in the everyday encounter of choices that we either lose our way or find our way on that magnificent path to greatness.

So don't let your vision goggles get clouded by the allure of good. God wants and has prepared for you a life of greatness, but you're the one who needs to choose and abide by it.

> My life changed the day I decided to never again run away from my comfort zone fears. When you think

about it, stepping through fear is a small price to pay
for a Big Dream. That one step- that we face many times
in our lives- must be the universal price tag that God
had in mind. I think God wants to know whether we
really want the wonderful gift of his Dream in our life.
—Bruce Wilkinson, *The Dream Giver*

God provides, you choose, and then you both spiritually partner in co-creating a Purpose PIE® path to greatness! It took me years and years to not just understand this principle but to actually apply it. My nature is to please others, and this created a monkey on my back and delayed the attainment of my life mission. If you find you have a similar monkey on your back, then let me let you in on a little secret of how to shoo that monkey away. Start to intentionally develop a keen desire to first and foremost please God each and every day. Get more confident and comfortable with saying no to the world and yes to God. And herein lies the paradoxical twist. As you learn to become more proficient and at peace with saying no to good, you will find that the temporary disappointment to others will be replaced with a far more impactful and life-changing difference in your legacy as you make your trek down the road to greatness that God has personally designed just for you.

Once we tune in completely to our spiritual voice, we start to sense the unfolding of unique and rare creativity by the Great Artist within. We become the brush of loving strokes in His hand to the bold new canvas of life that awaits us. Fear and uncertainty are slowly and gently replaced by faith. Many times the world is blind to our newfound vision that shines so radiantly for us in the distance. Yes, doubters and scoffers abound and the voice of impossible reverberates time and time again, yet we choose to move forward to the light of greatness anyway. We discover that we are all artists of creativity in our own right and have been assigned a mission-vision of daring dreams to bring into being.

> Artists are visionaries. We routinely practice a form of faith, seeing clearly and moving toward a creative goal that shimmers in the distance-often visible to us, but invisible to those around us.
>
> —Julia Cameron, *The Artist's Way*

I will never forget the day I met an intellectual property attorney that was referred to me by a friend. I needed his expertise to register a trademark for the words *Purpose PIE*®. I will never forget the look he gave me and his initial response as I shared my vision with him. He immediately had this bewildered look about him and appeared as if he was in pain as he enunciated, "Pur-pose ... PIE ... as in P-I-E?"

"Yes, sir," I answered as he looked at me as if I had been smoking something funny and right before him had sprouted another head on my body.

If there was one thing I knew for certain that day, it was this: when it came to my vision of Purpose PIE®, he was as blind as a bat to it. Don't get me wrong. He was an extremely nice and helpful professional who was happy to take my money that day for services rendered. It's just that as I was walking to my car after our transaction, I had the strangest feelings of dichotomy. In one sense I was so ecstatic about my vision, and yet I was bummed out as this intellectual property expert had confirmed indirectly that my daring dream was about as unrealistic and broken as one could possibly imagine. But luckily, after a few minutes I decided to chalk it up as an innocent misunderstanding. I knew right then and there I was not about to allow anything or anyone pry my dream away from me. I was confident in knowing that what

I lacked, God would more than make up the difference in making my dream take flight.

So let your imagination take flight and soar. Start dreaming and believing in what can be. Realize that good isn't good enough anymore. When the world whispers to you, "Oh no, that can't be done. Oh no, that's impossible. Oh no, you're not adequate enough," tell yourself YOLO! Yeah, YOLO applies to all of us: You Only Live Once!

Just knowing this truth should give us the raw determination to fight through good and into the land of greatness.

> You only live once, but if you do it right, once is enough.
> —Mae West, actress

Think you're not adequate enough to fit the bill of greatness? Then think again! Because you're not just shortchanging yourself and others; you're shortchanging God! You're living an illusion. So please do yourself a world of good favor and give up that thought right now. As much as you may think you want to live a daring dream to greatness, God wants it for you even more! He has just the perfect size and fit of vision goggles waiting for you. But you're the one who has to choose to put them on and to keep them on. And for those who fall in the camp of, "I'm too old for this to happen," then think again. Colonel Sanders was sixty-five when he took a family recipe and began franchising restaurants to serve fried chicken. Benjamin Franklin didn't invent bifocals until he was seventy-eight. Winston Churchill was also seventy-eight when he wrote a book that won the Nobel Prize for Literature. Nelson Mandela was inaugurated president of South Africa at age seventy-five. And Michelangelo didn't even begin his timeless masterpiece on St. Peter's Basilica until he was seventy-two. The list goes on and on. So don't fall for that terrible untruth.

You are never too old to set another goal or to dream a new dream.

—C. S. Lewis, author

A man is not old enough until regrets take the place of dreams.

—John Barrymore, actor

Become very sensitive and in tune with your daily decision making. Be brutally honest with yourself. Do you have some shoring up to do with your energy and time spent on "good"? Isn't it about time to have and carry out some daring dreams of your own? I certainly think it is. When you do, you will find that God will be right along your side on the journey to your rightful destiny. Then like me, you too will meet face-to-face the Colly of your impossible, daring dreams.

CHAPTER 9

Inner Peace

We all have heard the popular saying, "If you don't have your health, you don't have anything!" I agree with this statement to a degree because our health is such an integral part to the quality of our daily living. But I feel a far more accurate statement of truth would be, "If you don't have inner peace, you don't have anything!" See, I know, and I'm sure you also know, people who seem to have everything going on for them and are not just restless within but are downright miserable. Many can lay claim to good looks, wealth, great health, and worldly acclaim and yet have zero inner peace. I will tell you this fact of life: you will never, ever acquire total inner peace from the world and all the enticing trappings it has to offer. That can *only* come from one source: the Author and Creator of peace.

> For God is not a God of disorder but of peace.
> (1 Corinthians 14:33 NIV)

For me, I receive a daily dose of numinous nutrition that expands and safeguards my inner peace when I recite the "Serenity Prayer." As I incorporate this in my morning quiet time, I find that it gives me great comfort and strength in preparing for the emotional arrows of life that fly my way. I'm confident if you whisper this reverent prayer and receive it with an open heart and mind, it will soothe your soul also.

Serenity Prayer

God grant me the serenity
to accept the things I cannot change;
courage to change the things I can;
and the wisdom to know the difference.

When you emotionalize these beautiful words of truth, you can't help but start to get peaceful and grounded in the presence of God. It will help to keep you living in the present. When you live in the *present*, this is always a glorious *gift to behold.*

If you are depressed, you live in the past. If you are anxious you live in the future. But if you are at peace, you live in the present.

—Lao Tzu, philosopher

After nearly three decades as a risk manager in the beautiful state of Florida, I have witnessed many natural disasters. When Mother Nature comes rumbling through and leaves its pile of destruction behind, I've made an observation about the nature of people. In times of calamity, it brings out the worst in people, and it also brings out the very best in people. I've seen over and over again where many allow their values, integrity, and common courtesy to fly away with the prevailing winds. Others, I might add, somehow find calm within all the crazy calamity. In fact, some exude compassion and even demonstrate bold and heroic feats.

When I reflect on this further, I see some interesting parallels between nature and the nature of human beings. Some people respond as if they were a tornado, while some respond as if they were a hurricane. Let me explain. The entire makeup of a tornado is all about total turmoil and swirling chaos. A hurricane is similar but very different. Unlike a tornado, a hurricane has an eye or center that remains in a peaceful and serene state, regardless of outer circumstances. People respond in like fashion as either a tornado or hurricane when the winds of adversity strike.

Alexander Solzhenitsyn responded with calm, centered resolute as he faced extreme adversity in his life. For eight years he suffered in horrible conditions of prison for making negative comments about Joseph Stalin. I find it fascinating that he went to prison as an atheist and came out of prison as a Christian. This is how he described his challenging ordeal.

> I bless you prison—I bless you for being in my life—for there lying on rotting prison straw, I learned the object of life is not prosperity as I had grown up believing, but the maturing of the soul.

Although we are not in control or responsible for most life events and circumstances, we are responsible for how we react to them through our power to choose. Many times the emotional path chosen will determine the course of a person's entire life. We need to always attempt to recognize that there is purpose and meaning behind our painful circumstances. It's not easy, but we need to become very intentional in our act of faith as we choose to continue to trust and love God in spite of life's difficult and harsh lessons.

One life that exemplified steadfast faith in the midst of countless personal tragedies was that of Horatio G. Spafford. He demonstrated awe-inspiring inner peace despite suffering from waves of devastating life storms. In the late 1860s Horatio and his wife, Anna, lived with their five children in Chicago. Horatio had a successful law practice, and most of his wealth was invested in real estate by the shore of Lake Michigan. He also was a Presbyterian church elder and very active in many church and community projects. Up to this point in their lives, the Spafford family led a charmed life. Life was good. Then in 1870 tragedy struck. The Spaffords' four-year-old son, Horatio Jr., died of scarlet fever. They were devastated by the loss of their son. Then in October of 1871 the Great Chicago fire broke out, and most of the Spaffords' holdings were destroyed. Even though most of their finances were depleted, Horatio and Anna helped feed the hungry and assisted the homeless in their grief-stricken city.

The Spaffords befriended evangelists Dwight L. Moody and Ira D. Sankey and in 1873 had planned a trip to Europe to help assist them in a revival they were conducting in England. Due to business reasons, Anna and their four daughters were to set sail first, and then Horatio would follow on another ship a few days later. Then on November 22, 1873, the ship Anna and their four daughters were on was hit by a British iron sailing ship, and only 81 of 307 passengers and crew members survived the shipwreck. Anna luckily survived, but all four of the Spafford daughters had drowned. As soon as Horatio received Anna's telegram, he set sail to bring her home. It was near the crash site one night with Horatio alone in his cabin where he penned the words to his famous hymn, "It Is Well with My Soul." This is the first verse:

> When peace, like a river, attendeth my way,
> When sorrows like sea billows roll;
> Whatever my lot, Thou has taught me to say,
> It is well, it is well, well with my soul

After their reunion in Europe, Horatio and Anna returned to Chicago to begin their lives again. Several years later the Spaffords were blessed with three more children. They had another son and two daughters. In honor of their lost son, they named their new son Horatio. And just like his brother before him, when little Horatio turned the age of four, he also died of scarlet fever. Shortly after the Spaffords and a few of their friends left America for Israel and started a work that later became known as the American Colony. There they served the needy, helped the poor, cared for the sick, and took in homeless children.

When I first read about the lives of the Spafford family, I was sitting with my wife on our porch. We had recently experienced some disappointment and challenges of our own, and it was weighing heavy on our hearts. When I finished the article, I remember feeling embarrassed for my earlier feelings as I shared with Patti, "We don't have any problems!" It's amazing how being aware of other people's obstacles and setbacks can give you an entirely new perspective on yours. It's touching to me that the gargantuan and recurring tragedies in Horatio Spafford's life, were still not able to deter him from benefiting and experiencing inner peace. He became like the eye of a hurricane in keeping a calm, peaceful state within the center of his being with chaos and devastation all around. His soul was well not because he was void of conflict in the outer world but because he focused his awareness inward and kept his eye on God. Pain certainly hit Spafford and hit him hard and often, but he probably viewed continuous suffering as an option that didn't have to be once he chose to take refuge in God!

> Keep me safe, O God, for in you I take refuge. (Psalm 16:1 NIV)

Spafford was not devoid of harsh adversity, but he certainly decided to not let it define or control him. It became well with his soul because he rested his bruised and battered heart not in the outer, stormy circumstances of life but in the only place that any of us can ever hope to have any true inner peace: the resting place of God.

> You have made us for yourself, O God, and our hearts
> are restless until they find their rest in you.
> —St. Augustine

One day I witnessed firsthand when tragedy knocked for the third time on the door of a brokenhearted father and how he still demonstrated unwavering inner peace. I was attending a business meeting, and before it started I was standing next to a copier machine, making copies of some documents when I overheard a conversation between two business colleagues of mine. Jim had just entered the office, and a few days before he and his wife had just buried their third child. A friend spotted Jim entering and went over to him to provide some consolation. I then heard his friend say, "Jim, I'm sorry for your loss. If something like that happened to my two boys, what little faith I have, I'd end up with no faith at all."

Then I experienced one of the most poignant and tender moments in my lifetime. As Jim assessed his friend's comment, he took a deep breath, and his eyes watered. As he placed his right hand on his friend's shoulder, he said, "My friend, I want you to know that *because* of my faith I'm able to get through this, and if it wasn't for my faith I'd *never* get through it."

Unfortunately, many of the young lives in Jim's and Horatio's lives were cut short. But remarkably, just like a hurricane with chaos and calamity all around, the center of their being remained calm and peaceful as their chosen faith remained steadfast in God. God certainly understood the depth of their tragic pain as He once lost a precious Child too. One thing for certain is that we all come into the world to die someday. But far more important than the days we are given are the ways in which we give and live within those days.

> Be life long or short, its completeness depends on what
> it was lived for.
> > —David Stan Jordan, educator and writer

Life is a very fleeting moment in time. We all have different-sized windows of time. The real beauty, however, is not in the length or size of our window of time but whether our window is shining or not. So how's the shine on your window of time? Do others find it sparkling with a radiant glow and beauty? Or would they see it as a bit lackluster?

> Many people's tombstones should read: Died at thirty,
> buried at sixty.
> > —Nicholas Butler, philosopher

So if you feel you need a little buffing to spruce up your shine, then I'd like to share some thoughts with you about your window of time.

That Dash in the Middle
Steve Douglas

We come in the world to die someday,
From the moment of our birth 'til we leave this earth.
From our very first cry 'til that one last breath,
This becomes our window of life to death.
One thing common on our gravestones,
When we leave this life and when we leave alone,

We all have numbers to the left and right.
They're chiseled somewhere at our gravesite.
But that one little thing, the most important part of all,
That dash in the middle will say it all.
When it's all said and done and you're at the end of your line,
Did you live like you were dying? Did you love your ride?
Or the whole time living, were you dying inside
'Cause of all the bad choices and nowhere to hide?
That dash in the middle will say it all?
Did you give to many or none at all?
Did you live with love and have a grateful heart?
Or were you angry and bitter? You choose the part.
Was your dash about others ... or me, myself and I ...
Did you reach your potential? Did you even try?
Did your dash make some magic with kindness and grace,
Or did selfishness and harshness take their place?
Yeah, that little dash that looks so small,
If you dig a little deeper, it will tell it all.
How'd you play your song of life? Was it your true love?
Did you hold it tight, like a Stradivarius,
Playing it oh so sweetly all through the night?
Or did you take it for granted and play it second fiddle?
Only your dash can answer that riddle.
In the autumn of your years did you pay it forward
And plant shade trees, or were you so busy taking
It wasn't meant to be?
Did you honor and respect your gift of life,
Or did you show indifference morning, noon, and night?
Did it really matter that you lived at all?
Did your dash make a difference? That's for others to call.

Oh, that little dash is more than one thin line
'Cause it will speak volumes 'til the end of time.
God has given dashes from the beginning of time.
When He takes yours back, how will He see that line?
Will it shine like a star in the heavens at night?
Or will it bring Him sadness of a wasted life?
Oh that little dash is not so small after all.
I pray that your dash will shine for all.
Oh, how I pray it will shine for all.

Yes, I truly pray that your dash, your window of time, is shining brightly. Our Creator has created billions of stars, and He has a spot reserved just for you in His galaxy of shiny light. You just need to start trusting in the mystery of the journey. Turn a deaf ear to your voice of phony chatter, and start to trust the only one that matters. When your trust deepens, you will develop a daily rhythm of intuitive intervals. You will experience an ebb and flow of praying (speaking to God) and meditation (listening to God) in carrying out the labor of love accordingly. You begin to relish solitude as never before because it is here, in that time and space of quiet, that you receive your assignment and assuredness that your best work awaits you. Fear and trepidation melt into a calm and confident expectation as the whisper of your calling leads you out of noise and chaos and takes you into the joyful bliss of oh my goodness!

> Without great solitude, no serious work is possible.
> —Pablo Picasso, artist

You sense that the quiet that you choose to manifest will be your safe, undisturbed resting ground for receiving the sacred answers you seek. It is in that divine companionship of communication where discernment is given birth. Conformity to the ways of the world starts to loosen its stranglehold on you. You start to witness firsthand that it truly is in your very best interest to carry out God's will for you. It finally hits home that all the stuff of the world just doesn't work anymore. In fact, it never did. It's just that you didn't know it until now. You see, all that noise and senseless chatter was drowning out the voice of perfect love—the voice that really matters.

Ultimately, what really matters is to live a purposeful life in carrying out the daily will of God through your personally designed mission. In doing so you become totally centered with inner peace because you are generating your labor of love in something that is enduring and eternal. Disenchantment starts to set in with the temporary. Things that have been the backbone to your perceived happiness are starting to slouch and stoop a bit. Surprisingly, the allure of the carnal is beginning to lose its shimmer. A new light begins to emerge. A new path, a new way, a new life is offered, and now stands before you. The train of inner peace is now boarding, and it has a seat available, just for you. You can leave all your baggage of restlessness at the train station of life and take a ticket to finding rest in Him. God will be our conductor on our journey. The trip will become enduring as the final destination takes us to the land of Eternal Ville. And it brings me great joy and bliss to inform you that I've been assigned a seat right next to yours, as I will be with you all along the way. Oh, one more thing—I've been instructed to tell you fasten your seat belt! Your emotional seatbelt, that is.

CHAPTER 10

Enduring Joy and Bliss

So I ask you, where are you on the meter of contentedness? I don't think any of us will have a perfect ten each and every day until our next life. There are probably a few who grade out in the nines most of their days. But if there is one thing I am certain of, it is this: the ones who experience this healthy and vibrant emotional state of mind are not contingent upon happiness playing a role with their inner delight. People in this camp adhere to the enduring qualities that joy and bliss have to offer. You see, joy and bliss are all about choices. Happiness is dependent on things, stuff, situations, and circumstances. Happiness relies mightily on all kinds of contingencies. But I ask you, what happens when things break, rust, and wear out? What happens when finances are challenged, health deteriorates, and loved ones die? Happiness depends on happenings. Joy and bliss run deeper and stronger and are enduring and eternal in nature. It places its faith and trust in God. And in that faith and trust comes a quiet confidence that God will ultimately deliver on all of His promises.

> Then will I go to the altar of God, to God, my joy and
> my delight. (Psalm 43:4 NIV)

For me, happiness is all about "Having A Passing Pleasure In Never Enough Shiny Stuff." Yeah, we get our pleasure fix for a moment, but it never fails. Happiness will surely pass just as the wind is sure to come and go. Yes, we get a good jolt of happy when we get a raise, put on new clothes, and hop in our new car. But then it hits us one day. Some hard-to-describe feeling falls upon us with the strange sensation that something is missing. There's a void somewhere—an emptiness we just can't quite put our finger on. This black space that has meandered into our being is as real and certain as we are certain of our name.

> Man, I know all these things are supposed to seem important to us—the car, the condo, our version of success—but if that's the case, why is the general feeling out there reflecting more impotence and isolation and desperation and loneliness?
> —Brad Pitt, actor, *Rolling Stone Magazine* interview

Then one morning we catch our pretty new sweater on the car door and it's ruined as we hop in our shiny new car and notice that our yummy new car smell has hit the road, without even a good-bye. As we're driving to work, we are taken by surprise that out of the blue, dread and angst have taken residence in the pit of our stomach. It dawns on us that in a matter of months, our so-called dream job has shifted to a scream sob as what was once our respite to stimulation has now flowed into a cesspit of debilitation. Then reality hits, and it hits hard. The worldly stuff is no longer cutting the mustard. Then we tell ourselves for the very first time, "There just has to be a better way."

> Here I am in the twilight of my life, still wondering what it is all about ... I can tell you this, fame and fortune is for the birds.
> —Lee Iacocca

And guess what? There is a much better way, and I want to share the truth and beauty of it with you. The perfect antidote to your "happiness" dis-ease is to partake in a large dose of joyful bliss each and every day. And here's the deal. You can only get this life-saving prescription from one source.

> Here is the foundational truth that each of us needs to remember: *God is the only true source of joy.* God will be there when all else is shaking. He will be there when the people you love let you down or leave you or die. He will be there when the place you thought would make you happy doesn't satisfy any longer. He will be there when the possession is lost or gets broken. He will be there when your position changes or is given to someone else. He will be there when your personality just isn't enough.
>
> —Kay Warren,
> *Choose Joy, Because Happiness Isn't Enough*

Yes, God and God only supplies joyful bliss. He will furnish all you need of it in this life and the next. But you still have to choose it. And the best way to get off the taxing happiness wheel is to choose to trust and have faith in God that He will fill in all the empty, throbbing spaces that this world will never be able to provide. Out of faith and trust in God comes joyful bliss that becomes deeply rooted within the fabric of our lives. We are transformed into a passionate longing for the intimate and enduring pleasure of being in God's presence.

> When you do something from your soul, you feel a river moving in you, a joy.
>
> —Rumi, poet

The way that I look at it, BLISS is all about: Becoming Love's Inspired Sweet Spot. Our sweet spot is God's mission for us within our purposes. We are changing and becoming awe inspired as God is literally breathing newfound life into our beings. We are expanding in love from the one who created love and is love, the same one who died for love, lives for love, and knows our name ... all because of love. You just can't get away from the cold hard facts. Happiness feeds on circumstances, situations, things, and stuff. However, when you enter a BLISSFUL state, you begin to feed on love: Believing Life's Inner Sweet Spot Feeds Upon Love.

Think about it. When you're carrying out your labor of love (mission), you are demonstrating love to your Creator and giving love through service to your fellow man. And in so doing, you receive love in the form of inner peace, bliss, and fulfillment. It's the age-old giving-receiving principle at work in its finest hour.

Each and every day we have a critically important choice to make. Do we do our work or God's work? Do we remain in the happiness-seeking tribe that forever makes camp in the land of instant gratification? Do we accept a life of effectiveness when all the while our voice that matters awaits our emotional hand to take us into the realm of greatness? Stephen R. Covey was spot on when he determined that our lives become transformed from effectiveness to greatness "when we find our voice and inspire others to find theirs." It is on this path where our voice lays the stepping stones for us to step on the greatness that lies within. It is here where true and lasting love takes center stage every step of the way, and it is here where we inspire others to find their voice and ultimate BLISS (Becoming Love's Inspired Stepping Stones) so that they too may now step up to the stepping stones of greatness in *really* living to their full potential.

Living wide awake is about realizing that the world needs you to live up to your potential. There are others whose lives and futures depend, on you stepping up to accept your life's calling and responsibility, and then to create it. The future needs you to dream God-sized dreams; these are the only kind God gets involved in. And if the future needs anything, it is God working through people.

—Erwin Raphael McManus,
author, *Wide Awake: The Future Is Waiting within You*

Some heed the call; some don't. When your temporal pleasure is derived from the world, many times your judgement becomes clouded in making poor decisions. And many times those poor, impatient decisions come with serious and painful consequences. I'm sure we all have a few tucked away in our life experiences that we could share with each other. I'll share one of mine with you. One of the many jobs I had as a young boy was serving Cokes in an auditorium of a wrestling rink. I would fill all the cups with Coke and then load them in a steel carrying tray and then venture off into the crowd, selling my wares to the thirsty wrestling fans as the matches were going on.

One night, right at the end of the event it was extremely busy, and the last run always ended with me taking the Coke tray and sales proceeds back to our work station. Once we left both in their designated areas, then my work was completed and I could then venture home. This one night, however, I decided to leave the Coke tray, but I conveniently forgot to leave the proceeds, which were approximately seven or eight dollars.

You know how we eventually will have thousands of days in our lives that we can't remember a thing about? I will tell you this—that next day is a day that I will never, ever forget. The next morning our phone rang, and my father answered it. At first, it appeared as though it was just like any other normal call, and then I realized my dad was having a discussion with the man who owned the Coke concession. And it wasn't friendly chit-chat. They were talking about some missing money from the night before. That was the first time I realized that not abiding by your moral compass (conscious) could possibly make your heart feel and act like it would be much happier outside your chest cavity rather than in it. When my dad hung up the phone, he came over to where I was sitting and asked me, "Do you know anything about this missing money?"

It's funny how the desire for instant gratification at times muddies sound judgement but also clear and truthful answers. I knew the honest answer was a simple yes, but I just couldn't muster up the courage to say it. So instead I said, "Let me go check my blue jeans and see if I forgot about it." Forgot about it? Are you kidding me? Now I was not only a thief but also developing into a masterful storyteller, a.k.a., liar. And what do you know? The money had somehow magically ended up in one of my blue jeans pockets. Life lesson ... and moral of this story. Instant gratification isn't all it's cracked up to be, especially when you take something that's not yours! Even if it is all yours and you're caught in the perpetual buy-to-fulfill trap, this too will eventually have an empty and hollow feel to it.

There was a popular bumper sticker a few years ago: Too Much Ain't Enough.

> Too much ain't enough, and too soon is too late.
> The amateur, the addict and the obsessive
> all want what they want *now*. The corollary
> is that, when they get it, it doesn't work.
> The restlessness doesn't abate, the pain

> doesn't go away, the fear comes back
> as soon as the buzz wears off.
> —Steven Pressfield, *Turning Pro*

Fast forward a few decades, and one day my wife and I were taking our dog, Rusty, to the vet for some surgery. Rusty came through with flying colors and all was well. Our bill was around $700 to $800. I paid our bill with a credit card. When my statement came in the next month, my vet bill was not on it. I thought that it must have missed the cutoff for the monthly billing cycle. The next month's statement was also void of the pertaining charge, so I called the credit card company, and they confirmed there was no charge by my vet's office for that particular day. I then called the vet's office, and they stated my account was in good standing. When I explained the situation in fine detail, they said they would do some research and get back with me.

What I found out was interesting. The day we were in the vet's office, they experienced a serious rain and electrical storm. It had knocked out their computers and with it, all the daily activities and billing. This office had three or four vets working in it, so there were thousands of dollars of fees generated that went undetected. Once they became aware of the snafu, they were able to trace all transactions and bill accordingly. Could I have used the extra $700 or $800 in my checking account? Sure. But what if I just laid low and they were never to know what happened? The problem is, I would still know! Two voices. Two choices. Choose wisely. Sleep well and keep a healthy heart. And by the way, I received an awesome thank you from the vet's office.

The way I see it, happiness is really an adult pacifier! Babies eventually outgrow their dependency on them. We as adults should do the same. As children many of us played the game, "Let's pretend." As adults we play another pretend game. It just happens to go by the name of happiness. The child's game is far more relevant and significant in that they are at least exercising their imagination. The adult game many times is a waste of resources, time, and energy, which all lead to temporary pacification. This sort of lifestyle will never provide authentic sustenance for the very real need of fulfillment. Situations, circumstances, things, and stuff will never give you enduring and eternal satisfaction. Only God can do that for you. You see, God owns that game.

> But the plans of the Lord stand firm forever, the purposes of this heart through all generations. (Psalm 33:11 NIV)

> What does not satisfy when we find it was not the thing we were desiring.
>
> —C. S. Lewis

So what is the true joy to life? Hopefully you're starting to get a feel for your own personal answer to that extremely important question. For me, George Bernard Shaw hit the nail on the head with his.

> This is the true joy to life, the being used for a purpose recognized by yourself as a mighty one ... the being a force of nature instead of a feverish, selfish little clod of ailments and grievances complaining that the world will not devote itself to making you happy.

Wow! Mr. Shaw kind of summed up this joy, bliss, and happiness thing. It is my great hope that once you discover your mighty purpose, you will never give up under any circumstance to the attainment of that loving, sacred call. You will need faith, grit, and determination as you wade through your everyday encounter of life. You will need to call upon a great warrior and true friend to the noble cause of purpose. You need to be totally devoted and trusting to this very loyal friend who has been waiting to help you in your quest to bring your calling to the world. No, her name is not Lady Luck. Her name is Lady Persistence. And I can't wait for the two of you to get to know each other as never before. You'll be *a lot* more than happy that you did!

CHAPTER 11

Never Give Up

The human spirit hungers for the discovering, expressing, and fulfilling of one's calling in life. Unfortunately, once you commence in this purposeful pilgrimage, you will encounter obstacles and roadblocks along the way. Do not allow these temporary detours to thwart your magnanimous endeavor in any way. Look at them as bumps in the road. Persist at all costs to keep your calling nurtured and untethered.

Welcome Lady Persistence as your new and noble friend as you journey on this magnificent quest. As you partner and befriend Lady Persistence, she will ultimately deliver the goods. She will make and bake you a one-of-a-kind pie, a Purpose PIE® high! She will create a playground of passion, inspiration, and enthusiasm to the likes of which you have never had the pleasure to play in. Remember, in creating your own true, unique, and authentic Purpose PIE®, Lady Persistence is an ingredient of paramount proportion. It needs to be added and applied daily, and an extra pinch or two will be just fine. Know full well that it is God's design for us to live with purpose. Once you discover it, invite Lady Persistence to be your daily playmate in your labor of love. She will aid you in releasing the creative inner child within. Let yours come out and play, and play often. When a few unexpected stumbling blocks appear, just view them as mere spiritual stepping stones. Be steadfast in confidence that God's purpose for you cannot and will not be diminished, dismantled, or defeated.

> I know that you can do all things: no plan of yours can
> be thwarted. (Job 42:2 NIV)

Remember, we no longer operate and function from the ego but of the Spirit. And because we have chosen to spiritually *partner in relational intimacy together*, we need to keep our end of the bargain alive and well. We need to show up each and every day and do the work. No matter what amount of unexpected difficulty lies before us, we press on. We press on because we learn that persistence is a powerful force when called upon. It breaks down walls and seemingly impenetrable barriers. It turns impossible right on its head to the possible. It will cut a no down to its knees and make a yes sound that will please. It is a life-changing agent like no other and a life force to be reckoned with when used with unwavering determination. It trumps talent, genius, and education in ways that defy logic and reason. Lady Persistence is truly one of the greatest gifts God has ever given to man.

Some of us have had or will have many jobs and careers in our lifetime. All of us have one calling in our life. I've had countless jobs, but once I received my education, I've had two careers.

Before my career in risk management and fresh out of college, I began a career as a sales representative in the fine printing paper industry. I sold hundreds of different types of papers with varied colors, weights (thickness), and textures. I called on printing companies, newspapers, book publishers, companies, universities, municipalities, etc., that performed printing in house. I worked straight commission and covered all of my business expenses. I viewed it as a plateful of opportunity with no free lunch. I made cold calls often and received some form of rejection daily for thirteen years. I loved the people I worked for and had the utmost respect and admiration for them.

The first couple of years were a real struggle for me. I could clearly see the long-term potential, but typically it was extremely difficult to break into many of these accounts. Most of them had their established vendors that they had conducted business with for years. Because of this, relationships ran deep, thus making protective moats of entry tough on a young greenhorn like myself.

Suddenly, I found myself right smack dab in the middle of the school of hard knocks. That knock of reality was not very pretty. In fact it was downright painful. Beanie weenies became a regular staple on my daily menu of sustenance. Opportunity and potential are wonderful things, and so are eating and paying bills. I decided rather quickly that a second job would best serve me, so I worked nights and weekends selling men's clothing in a large retail store.

I was working such crazy hours just to try and make ends meet that my employer offered to expand my territory a bit. There was the beautiful sleepy little town of Deland, Florida, just west of where I had been concentrating my sales efforts. Immediately I was able to break into a couple new accounts, but I soon found out that the crown jewel of the area was Stetson University. They had their own captive shop on campus that supplied most of their printing needs for the university. I will never forget the first time I walked into their printing facility and made a quick assessment. There were pallets and pallets of cartons of fine printing paper everywhere. Some nearly went to the very high ceilings! Immediately I was thinking, *No more part-time job!*

As I introduced myself to a couple of the pressmen, I soon found out that the plant manager and buyer of all the paper orders was a man by the name of Mario Lossaso. My optimism meter was rising quickly, and I was truly stoked to meet this gentleman named Mario so I could tell him all the wonderful things my company and I could do for him. I found myself in front of him with an extended hand as I introduced myself. As soon as I finished my little introductory spiel, I received something in my memory bank now filed forever under the tab of rejection.

Mario looked at me straight in the eyes with such seriousness and such incredibly stern and uncompromising body language that it immediately started to short circuit my optimism meter. Then he said, "I'm sure you're a nice young man and you are working with a good company, but let me just say this the best way I know how. I will never, ever buy anything from you or your company ... never! I buy all my paper from one paper company, and their representative, Jim, is not only a true professional but also like a son to me. I can't tell you the number of times that he has helped pull me out of jams!"

My response to Mario was, "Well, Mr. Lossaso, I'm going to be in Deland every Wednesday servicing my new customers, so I sure would appreciate it if I could stop by and just stick my head in the door."

He replied, "If you want to waste your time, then go for it!"

As I was walking back to my car like a hurt and dejected puppy, I was thinking it would be next to impossible for me to ever break into this account. I was thinking my second job was probably going to have to hang around quite a bit longer.

And then it happened! Just a few days after this experience, I was conversing with one of my customers as he was finishing the printing of an order. When he finished he handed me the last page and said I could keep it if I wanted to. His press run was a quote entitled "Press On," by Calvin Coolidge.

> Nothing in the world can take the place of persistence. Talent will not; nothing is more common that unsuccessful men with talent. Genius will not; un-rewarded genius is almost a proverb. Education will

not; the world is full of educated derelicts. Persistence and determination alone are omnipotent.

Well, when I finished reading this famous quote for the first time, I immediately felt that I had just received a Godwink as to how I was going to eventually break into the protective moat of impossible. When I got home that day, I scotch taped this quote on a wall in my clothes closet. Every time I went into my closet to get dressed for the day, I would read that quote out loud, over and over and over again. I decided right then and there that I would never, ever quit calling on Mario Lossaso under any circumstances. Lady Persistence and I had befriended each other, and we became loyal and trusted friends of one another.

Fast forward several months, and like clockwork I had made my weekly call of rejection without missing a beat. The more I read that quote, the more determined I became to *never give up!* Now I was into a half year, then seven months, eighth months, and nine months. At the end of the ninth month, I was entering the Stetson University print shop, and soon as I walked in, I saw two of the press operators laughing hysterically. I assumed one of them had shared a joke or funny story with the other. As I greeted both of them, I asked them if they could share with me what was the cause of their laughter, as I could certainly have stood a laugh considering where I was at that very moment.

Then Jim spilled the beans and said, "Steve, as soon as you walked in the door we just started howling. Jack and I have been making bets on you for months on how long it would be before you quit calling on us. We can't tell you the number of reps that quit calling after a week or so. But you are unbelievable. You are relentless! You just *never* give up!"

Before I could even respond to their keen observation, I saw Mario at the far end of the building, and he appeared to be waving me over to where he was. As I walked over and said, "Good morning," he appeared very stern as he was taking off his printer's apron. He then said matter of factly, "Come with me."

Immediately the movie *The Godfather* came to mind, and I was thinking maybe this persistence thing had caused me to wear out my welcome and my end was near. He motioned me into his private office to come in and sit down. Not saying a word, he turned his swivel chair and reached for a printing papers catalog. As he was flipping through the pages of his printer's manual and without looking at me, he asked me a question that will forever be emblazoned in every fiber of my being. He said, "Do you have nine-by-twelve, twenty-four-pound white wove catalog envelopes?"

I quickly replied, "Yes, sir!"

Then he looked at me and said, "Send me ten thousand of them on your next truck ... Now get your a** out of here!"

As I walked to my car, I was physically shaking with excitement! I realized right then and there that statements of "never, ever" work on a lot of things. In fact, just about everything ... other than Lady Persistence. Persistence and determination are truly omnipotent. And my dear friend, I want you to own and experience this spiritual truth on your quest to fulfilling your calling.

> Permanence, perseverance, and persistence in spite of all obstacles, discouragements and impossibilities: It is this that in all things distinguishes the strong soul from the weak.
> —Thomas Carlyle, philosopher

> Energy and persistence conquer all things.
> —Benjamin Franklin, inventor

> Survival can be summed up in three words: never give
> up. That's the heart of it really! Just keep trying.
>   —Bear Grylls, adventurer

Yeah, Lady Persistence really does deliver the goods. And she delivered a lot more than just those ten thousand envelopes. She eventually had my different brand of papers stacked everywhere you can imagine in that place of impossible—some nearly touching that very high ceiling! I'm sure you guessed it ... good-bye, second job. Mario and I developed not only a professional relationship but also a genuine friendship.

From this personal experience, a life lesson was yelling at me loud and clear. The by-product and what later became the cornerstone of perseverance is one thing. And that one thing is *respect*! As you are persevering through your daily battles, the world may not want to do business with you, love you, like you, or even want to be around you. But there is one thing the world will do: it will be a tilt in your good favor. And it will come about as naturally as the earth's axis is naturally tilted in its daily movement. The offspring of good favor that is generated from ongoing persistence is that you will become *respected* and being RESPECTED is all about: Relentless Effort Serves People Extraordinary Chances To Experience Dreams.

Yes, daring dreams really can and do come true. And when you become respected, that priceless emotion that you create in others will oftentimes be the leverage needed to do the heavy lifting of the emotional drawbridge near the protective moat of impossible.

Lady Persistence finally has her day in court, and the scales of justice favor you. The dark clouds of no, never-ever, and impossible are opening now, and it is your time to revel in the sunshine of possible. It is here where you now see that placing your hopes and dreams in the safekeeping of Lady Luck is a loser's game. You see the truth. The truth is, there is nothing lucky or magical about becoming exemplary in persistence. You know what it takes. It takes guts, grit, and impenetrable faith in staying the course. That's why it's so highly respected. Most everyone knows and understands how it works, but very few are willing to pay the price to deliver the goods daily. Wishing and chasing Lady Luck around appear to be a much easier way to go. But wishing and placing all your bets on Lady Luck will not create the change agents required in delivering your mission to the world. It is only by partnering in co-creating with God and developing a bold and courageous resolve to persist at all costs that will lead you to the sacred ground of what can be.

> Luck is merely an illusion, trusted by the ignorant and chased by the foolish.
> —Timothy Zahn, science-fiction writer

There's just no getting around it. We have to do the work. We have to actively participate in making, shaping, and baking our Purpose PIE® before the world can feast on it. Can we truly love this creative process? Absolutely! So many hours and days just fly by because it oftentimes feels like play. But life's not perfect, and sometimes we encounter some bumps in the road on our sweet-spot pilgrimage. It's those days of unusual resistance when we need to pull something from within and become extra strong. Author Steven Pressfield describes this process beautifully:

> Two key tenets for days when resistance is really strong.
> Take what you can get and stay patient.
> The defense may crack late into the game
> Play for tomorrow.

Our role on tough-nut days is to maintain our composure and keep chipping away. We're pros. We're not amateurs. We have patience. We can handle adversity.

Tomorrow the defense will give us more, and tomorrow we'll take it.

There's a third tenet that underlies the first two:

We're in this for the long haul.

Our work is a practice.

One bad day is nothing to us. Ten bad days are nothing.

In the scheme of our lifelong practice, twenty-four hours when we can't gain yardage is only a speed bump. We'll forget it by breakfast tomorrow and be back again, ready to hurl our bodies into the fray.

And that's what I want to share with you next—how to equip yourself mentally, emotionally, and spiritually when you find yourself in the fray of adversity.

CHAPTER 12

Trusting God While Dancing in the Rain

Learn the alchemy true human beings know. The
moment you accept what troubles you've been given,
the door will open.

—Rumi

An inevitable truth of life that we all sooner or later have to come to
grips with is that life is difficult and we will face many challenging
storms throughout our existence. It is how we handle and react to
those life storms that will determine greatly the quality of life that we
will experience. Even when we are right on track with our calling and
are *really* living in the sweet spot of life, we will continue to encounter
conflictive struggles. No matter how healthy, wealthy, positive, or
peaceful we may be, we're all in the same boat rowing down the
same stream. The truth is, if we live long enough, we all get doled out
generous portions on our plate of difficulties. Unlike monopoly, no
one gets a get out of jail free card. We all carry our personal cross in
life, and some days it's much heavier than others. Even Christ didn't
sugarcoat this truth as He made no bones about it when He said in John

16:33, "In this world you will have trouble" (NIV). But He followed up on this harsh dose of reality with three words that emanate hope. Those three words were, "But take heart." It is the hope within those three words where I want to share some thoughts with you.

> Hardships often prepare ordinary people for an extraordinary destiny.
>
> —C. S. Lewis, author

Shortly after I realized how much peace and bliss I derived from the creative process of songwriting, I became intentional in wanting to write a song that paid tribute to God for seeing me through my adversities in life. I knew from the onset that I wanted the title of the song to be "My Power in My Pain." I have always loved music for as long as I can remember. I even played a little acoustic guitar and alto sax. I really wasn't that passionate about it because anytime I had available I would prefer listening to the artists who had already mastered their craft. When I started songwriting, I was totally blind and completely unaware of basic song structure protocol. I didn't have a clue what a verse, chorus, hook, bridge, or outro was. I winged it from the very sense of the word. But my sheer love for music and my fascination with how words can deeply move people gave me just enough lyrical ammo to be somewhat dangerous.

I decided to use some of these early and very raw forms of creativity in Purpose PIE®. I wanted to demonstrate that when one finds one's calling, there is a natural process of stumbling forward, but stumbling forward we must go. You will find, as I did, God will be there each and every time to pick you up and dust you off so that you can take heart for better days ahead. Like most things in life, once I began to put the necessary time and energy into this endeavor, I slowly but surely started advancing on the learning curve. Remember, any form of creativity in carrying out your calling has absolutely nothing to do with perfection. It's everything about evolving, growing, and becoming your true self.

> The thing that is really hard, and really amazing, is giving up on being perfect and beginning the work of becoming yourself.
>
> —Anna Quindlen

> There is a crack in everything. That's how the light gets in.
>
> —Leonard Cohen, "Anthem"

Countless people go to their graves every day without experiencing the wonder of playing out the calling of their mission due to the dreaded dis-ease of perfectionism. I say give yourself some slack and self-compassion and choose to feel comfortable with your cracks of perfect imperfections. After all, when we're operating from the Spirit, those cracks let the light of God in. When this form of *LIGHT* (Left In God's Hands Totally) comes in, then things begin to happen that we could never accomplish on our own.

> So many of us run around spackling all of the cracks, trying to make everything look just right. It reminds me that our imperfections are not inadequacies; they are reminders that we're all in this together. Imperfectly, but together.
>
> —Brene' Brown, *The Gifts of Imperfection*

It's funny, many people have asked me what actually prompted me to start writing. Was there a particular artist who influenced and inspired me to pursue this creative process? I guess the best answer would be that the Creator of all artists started prompting me in the early-morning hours. Many times I would wake up and a flood of ideas and thoughts would rush to me. Most of the time I felt compelled to get up and record these unexpected messages on paper. It was as if the world was in a deep slumber as I was being spoon-fed numinous nutrition in the quiet hush of early morning. It has been and continues to be a welcomed encounter that I find intimate and awe-inspiring.

> You never have to change anything you got up in the
> middle of the night to write.
>
> —Saul Bellow

From my song, "My Power in My Pain" I experienced many early promptings that came quick and often. In no time the verses and the chorus presented themselves. For several reasons I felt this particular song just had to have a bridge in it for it to be impactful and truly complete. For those of you not familiar with the lyrical term *bridge*, I'll share some basic tenets of its meaning. Often a bridge has contrasting melody and a new key. A bridge is typically used to pause and reflect on the earlier portions of the song or to prepare the listener for the climax. It can be helpful in breaking up a repetitive pattern of the song and keep listeners' attention. I call creating this nuance as making "ear candy." In addition to creating contrast from the rest of the song, it can provide deeper insight and meaning to what the song is really trying to convey to the listener and thus deliver far more impact.

Unfortunately, for the creation of the bridge I had just the opposite experience that I'd had with the ease that the chorus and verses flowed to me. It seemed to take forever! In fact, just over two and a half years, to be exact. Every time I'd come up with an idea for the bridge, I'd can it rather quickly as I knew there was just something missing. My writing, which usually brought me so much inner peace and bliss, was becoming taxing on my emotions to say the least! This bridge thing was truly turning my pleasure into my pain.

Then it hit me, just like the songs title made reference to, I needed to seek my Power and ask for help within my pain! I happened to be at our little getaway home. It was just me and Buckley, our adorable little tri-color Papillion dog. Patti had given me her blessings to find a space of quiet to write for a week as she was having her summer girls' time with her nieces.

My initial goal was to knock out the bridge in my song the first day and then devote the rest of my time to working on Purpose PIE®. Well, goals are great to have, but this particular goal had gone awry as I found myself going to bed at the end of the third day with a big nothing, nada, zip to show for all my efforts. I was frustrated beyond belief. And then it happened! I woke up at 2:30 a.m., and as I was reflecting on my earlier disappointment, I began to pray.

I found myself praying in a way that I was not accustomed to. I guess the best way to describe it was through sheer frustration, I finally threw down my creative gauntlet, so to speak. For the life of me, I just couldn't understand why God wasn't doing His part! Why on God's green earth would He not respond to my painful cry in wanting to create something beautiful that would pay homage to His greatness? I just didn't get it. It made no sense to me whatsoever, until just a few minutes after 4:00 a.m. When I looked at my bedroom clock and observed that it was 4:00 I thought, *Wow!* Never had I prayed so long and intently or meditated as fervently. I guess God had enough of my rambling as I now felt prompted to get out of bed. I left little Buckley belly up to the ceiling, snoring away. I then went into my reading-writing room, turned on a light, picked up my pen, and started writing. I wrote six lines in about three minutes or so. As I was writing, I wasn't fully conscious of what I was writing per se.

It seemed as though I was just writing instructional words with no rhyme or reason. When I finished, I put my pen down and picked up my notepad, and as I read those words, I remember shaking and crying uncontrollably. Not sad tears, mind you, but deliriously joyful-blissful tears. I knew right then and there that I had just experienced a beautiful and loving spiritual encounter.

> By day the Lord directs his love, at night his song is with me—a prayer to the God of my life. (Psalm 42:8 NIV)

I'm deeply honored to share with you the words that God so tenderly placed in my heart.

> "You know you taught me well, through all my prayers
> When You said these words to me
> Life's not fair and storms don't care, when they leave you full of pain
> But storms don't last and 'til they pass, go dancin' in the rain
> 'Cause the Power's in the dancer who's dancin' in the rain.
> Yeah, the Power's in the dancer who's dancin' in the rain"

Isn't God amazing! What I had toyed with for nearly three years and then painstakingly, laser-white intentionally concentrated on for three full days, all to no avail, God delivered in three intimate and wondrous minutes. And in those six lines, I felt that God was speaking volumes to me. He was saying, "Be persistent, resilient, and above all, faithful in the storms of life." No matter how many storms come our way with all the accompanying pain, continue to remain empowered by seeking out His Power.

My Power in My Pain©
Lyrics by: Steve Douglas

When storms are rollin' in and fear is breaking loose
You're my silver linin', You get me desirin'
To search and be with You
My calm before the storm, You make me so serene
You are the best of things, the best I've ever seen

When trouble comes knockin'... yeah, knockin' on my door
With danger all around
You rush to me, You keep me safe. You keep me safe and sound
You shower me with love. My Power from above
So still, but yet so deep. Your love is mine to keep

'Cause of love, You listen... You listen like a lake
You give... give... give to me. You give me what it takes
So much more than a friend, my strength to start again
Yeah, You are my power, my power in my pain

When the world is so cruel, I close my eyes and think of You
Breathe real deep, then I know, Your love will see me through
Dark days come crashin' in, get so sad. Get so blue
Then I go in my heart, and that's where I find You
Hold me close. Lift me up. You make me feel brand new

When people take and take, and wound with words of hate
You know I feel the fear. Want You close, want You near
'Cause I get the power, to look fear in the face
My fortress from the fray, my blue skies after gray
You are my peace within, true love that has no end

'Cause of love, You listen... You listen like a lake
You give... give... give to me. You give me what it takes
So much more than a friend, my strength to start again
Yeah, You are my power, my power in my pain

You know You taught me well, through all my prayers
When You said these words to me
Life's not fair and storms don't care, when they leave you full of pain
But storms don't last and 'til they pass, go dancin' in the rain
'Cause the power's in the dancer, whose dancin' in the rain
Yeah, the power's in the dancer, whose dancin' in the rain

'Cause of love, You glisten... You glisten like a lake
You shine... shine... shine on me. Your light is mine to take
So much more than a friend, You set me free again
'Cause of You, my power... I'm dancin' in the rain
Yeah, 'cause of You, my power... I'm dancin' in the rain
And in my darkest hour... with You... it's all ... for gain

So seek His *LIGHT* (Left In God's Hands Totally) in the lightning storms of life. Remain loving and trusting in God in each and every adversity downpour. Become soaked with His promises of enduring love and hope. Know full well that eventually He will make all things right, and one day all of our storms of life will be over and behind us forever. So revel in the moment, no matter the moment. Learn, grow, and evolve in a way that the world does not understand. In all kinds of weather, just bind together. Take the chance with sacred dance, for when the winds will surely blow, this truth you will dearly know. With passing storms and passing rain, when danced with Him, it has been ... all for gain.

> Search for the seed of good in every adversity. Master
> that principle, and you will own a precious shield that
> will guard you well through all the darkest valleys you
> must traverse. Stars may be seen from the bottom of
> a deep well, when they cannot be discerned from the
> mountain top.
>
> —Og Mandino, author

The way I see it, adversities are another opportunity to draw closer to God. With every life storm we all have important choices to make. We can *fight* our battles like a mighty oak against the heavy winds. We can take *flight* and withdraw quickly and quietly like a rolling tumbleweed. Or we can depend on LIGHT (Left In God's Hands Totally) to lead and guide us like a bending and resilient willow that dances lightly in the stormy wind and rain.

> The oak fought the wind and was broken, the willow
> bent when it must and survived.
>
> —Robert Jordan, *The Fires of Heaven*

We need to become very sensitive in how we choose to allow adversity to affect us. The adversity EFFECT (Everyone's Feelings Favoring Eggs-Carrots-Tea) all boils down to one of three choices. When the heat of adversity hits 212 degrees or higher, we take on one of three characteristics. We become like a boiled egg as we harden on the inside. We become like a cooked carrot in that we are firm and strong before the boiling point of adversity, yet we now discover that the very fiber of who we are has become soft and weak. Or we choose to be like tea leaves as we travel lightly to the boiling movement of adversity and by our sacred, rhythmic dance, we draw beautiful flavor and aroma from the very pain itself. We make honey from the sting in all that life will bring.

> We are like the herb which flourisheth most when trampled upon.
>
> —Walter Scott, *Ivanhoe*

When setbacks, disappointments, or tragedies come rumbling in, we many times choose to *disengage*. Like a cooked carrot, we become soft and weak inside. We lose our fortitude and courage. Some will choose to *rage* and become bitter and like the egg will harden inside. Others will find blessings within the mess and like the tea leaves, will make beauty from bad. They won't put up their umbrellas of disengaging and raging in the heavy downpour. But they most surely will *ENGAGE* (Edge Near God As God Edifies) in trusting to dance with God in the rain of pain. As they engage in drawing near to God, He will guide, develop, and enlighten them with a power that will always overcome their pain and transform beauty from brokenness.

> Our cup is often so full of pain that joy seems completely unreachable. When we are crushed like grapes, we cannot think of the wine we will become.
>
> —Henri Nouwen, *Can You Drink The Cup?*

When we learn to dance in the rain, we begin to take on spiritual and emotional mind-set of what Victor Frankl made reference to as "tragic optimism." We reach the capacity where we begin to find meaning in adversity. We find we no longer need to keep our loss hidden deep within the dark. In fact, we discover we no longer fear the dark. Because here, as we wait patiently on God with our open and broken hearts, we come to see the treasure in our trash and feel the plenty in our empty. We become broken open, and it is the trusting of openness to brokenness where we finally allow God to take us places where we could never go by ourselves.

> I had to make a decision, and you do too: Will I surrender to God in the darkness, believing that I will find treasures of joy, blessing and meaning here? Although I didn't like it, God had allowed me to be in that dark place. I had to decide whether I would embrace it so he could lead me to the treasures I could find only in suffering.
>
> —Kay Warren, *Choose Joy Because Happiness Isn't Enough*

Our quest for uncovering our true selves is the Phoenix Process. The Egyptians believed that every five hundred years the phoenix bird renewed his quest for his true self. Knowing that a new way could only be found with the death of his worn-out habits, the phoenix built a pyre of cinnamon and myrrh, sat in the flames, and burned to death. Then he rose from the ashes as a new being.

> Each one of us, regardless of our situation, is looking for the same treasure in the ashes. We are in search of our most authentic, vital, generous, and wise self. What stands between that self and us is what burns in the fire. Our illusions, our rigidity, our fear, our blame, our lack of faith and our sense of separation: All of these in varying strengths and combinations—are what must die in order for a more true self to arise. If we want to turn a painful event into a Phoenix Process, we must name what needs to burn within us.
>
> —Elizabeth Lessen, *Broken Open*

I've been burning some worn-out habits of my own of late—things like gaining approval of others, defensiveness, and wounding with words. What I have found is once we start the burn, we immediately start the Phoenix Process to healthy change. But not until we find ashes on our knees daily do we experience radical, permanent change in finding our ultimate treasure of knowing our true and authentic selves. Going all the way to the bottom of our ash heap and on our knees completes the downward spiral of allowing the death of all our illusions and fears. Once the ashes of what we no longer want to be are caked thick on our knees, we then can arise and be confident and gloriously grateful for finding our true selves of being in a loving, personal, and intimate relationship with God.

So what are some of your old, worn-out habits that need to burn so you can begin to venture down the path of discovering your true self? If we're truly honest, we all have some. We are steady works in progress. That's why it's so healthy to dance lightly like the willow. When we radiate this kind of light to the world, we experience understanding, compassion, and empathy that take us to a new and fresh realm of insight. We become courageous and fearless in a new and glorious way. We become tenderhearted and kind souls.

> Be kind. Everyone you meet is fighting a hard battle.
> —Philo of Alexandria

You know dancing in the rain isn't easy, but it sure is worthwhile. All you really need is a little GRIT^3: Godly Responses In Trials, Tribulations, Tragedy. So when your next storm of adversity comes rolling in, I want you to muster up some GRIT^3. And the very first thing all of us need to do within our GRIT^3 is to call upon our Power, our loving God. Grit is all about the tendency to sustain interest in an effort toward very long-term goals. When you think about it, there isn't a longer-term goal than to be with God. Hey. He created eternity, and it certainly doesn't get any longer than that!

When the pain of life rains upon you, remember:

1. Muster some GRIT^3 as you call upon God.
2. Engage in life with Light (Left In God's Hands Totally).
3. Be resilient like the willow.
4. Go dancing in the rain.
5. Make tea out of adversity.
6. Find bless within the mess.
7. Make some honey from the sting in all that life will bring.
8. Flower in the fray.

> The flower that blooms in adversity is the rarest and most beautiful of all.
> —*Mulan*, Walt Disney Co.

> It was time for me to step boldly into the fullness of life, with all of its dangers and all of its promises. Remaining tight in a bud had become kind of a death. The time had come to blossom.
> —Elizabeth Lesser, *Broken Open*

So, my trusting and faithful friend, thank you for staying with me. As we are coming to the end of our time together, you will soon begin your Purpose PIE® journey in discovering your true self. Now is the time for you to come out of your bud. Now is the time for you to blossom. There is no greater time than right now for you to unfold your sweet spot of magnificence. And it is time to discuss just that—time!

CHAPTER 13

Sense of Urgency

You may find it strange or funny, but for many years now I have scanned daily the obituary section of my local newspaper. My main intention is to observe all the people who have recently died who are my age and younger. This serves me well in that for starters, it keeps me humble and grateful. It keeps me humble in that it is my daily dose of reality that life is extremely fragile and it can come crashing down at any moment. It keeps me grateful in that I fully realize the truth that each one of those who have died God loved every bit as much as He loves me. And yet, they are now gone, and by the grace of God, I am still here. This daily visit with mortality keeps me very grateful. It also creates an urgency of doing. I feel a burning desire to complete my duty in carrying out my calling from God.

> I have been impressed with the urgency of doing. Knowing is not enough; we must apply. Being willing is not enough; we must do.
>
> —Leonardo da Vinci, artist

This daily revisit with fresh humility and gratitude helps keep me on task to carry out my calling and the sooner, the better! If I'm ever going to witness and fully experience the unfolding and blossoming of my daring dreams then that time is now. Not next month, next year, next whatever, but right now! And guess what? That time is for you also. Here's the reality. Every year that fades by, I take note that there are more people who continue to fall into this category. With each passing year, more and more folks keep showing up in the obit column who are my age or younger.

Remember my frog in the pond story? I see a great parallel here. The frog is unaware of the increasing degree as we become unaware of a passing day. But then that one degree turns to two, then five, then ten, and so on. And our day turns to a week, a month, a year, and on and on. Then one day that one extra degree comes about and that last day presents itself, and all of a sudden, you, I, and the frog are no longer here. You see, that's how time operates. What at first appears slow and abundant slowly but surely turns into fast and limited. There are a lot of things that are okay to be nonchalant about, but our time isn't one of them. We had better value it as one of our most precious assets because it is the framework wherein we create the story of our lives.

> There is no agony like bearing and untold story inside you.
>
> —Maya Angelo, poet

> Until you value yourself, you won't value your time. Until you value your time, you will not do anything with it.
>
> —M. Scott Peck, psychiatrist-author

So I say to you caringly, what kind of life story have you been creating? If you were to find out today that you had another month or two to live, would you honestly be at peace and completely satisfied with your story? I find it sad and deeply disturbing how there is such a gargantuan contrast among the stories of lives when I scan the daily obituary column. You read some, and you just know that a particular story would have made the great William Wallace proud as a peacock because it becomes obvious that they *really* lived. Many others not so, as these were the unfortunate souls that Thoreau made reference to as leading lives of quiet desperation.

The best way to describe a life story is not by ourselves but by others. How we loved, served, and impacted others or not will determine the story of our lives. When we depart this life, it will be others who will fill in the blanks in describing our brief existence. Yeah, it's that dash in the middle that says it all. So I say *memento mori*. Remember that you will die. If you allow it, death can become a great teacher and friend of ours because it can give deeper, richer meaning to life. When you live as though you face death all the time (because you do), you *really* begin to live. You can get white hot and on fire for discovering and delivering your calling before the opportunity is no more.

> Why, you do not even know what will happen tomorrow.
> What is your life? You are a mist that appears for a
> little while and then vanishes. (James 4;14 NIV)

Having a healthy relationship with death is the way to *really* come alive in daily living. When death is feared or pushed out far in one's thoughts, it impedes us from living full out.

> Endeavor to live so that when you die, even the
> undertaker will be sorry.
>
> —Mark Twain

When we fear the sting of death, our hearing becomes muffled to the ring of a sense of urgency. We begin to lose our way. We're not all in to carpe diem. We not only don't "seize the moment," but death seizes us ... *before* we die. We keep crawling for crumbs as the minutes keep running by. As we crawl and time runs by, this *metastasizes* the cancer to our calling. We become the judge, jailer, and executioner to the death of our fulfillment long before our lives have ended.

> This is your life and it's ending one minute at a time.
>
> —Chuck Palahnuik, writer

But when we allow death to become a great instrument in helping us play out our unique song of life, then the thing that ends our lives will be the very thing that makes us come alive within our lives.

> Remembering that I will be dead soon is the most
> important tool I've ever encountered to help me make
> the big choices in life.
>
> —Steve Jobs, Apple, cofounder

Years ago I created a concept that I call blocks of ten (ten years). This concept assists me in staying present in life with a great sense of urgency. I want to encourage you to do the same. Start viewing your life in terms of blocks of ten. Life expectancy in the United States has been trending upward for some time now. Currently the average expected age of a female is just over eighty years and a little under eighty for the average male.

To illustrate, let's say you're forty-five years old. That means according to the average life expectancy, you have already lived approximately four and a half blocks of your life and you have roughly three and a half blocks left. We all come to learn that with each passing year, it just seems to go by faster and faster. So I say to you, anything that's really important to you that you want realized and anything of paramount significance that you want fulfilled, then do the math. Emotionalize your own blocks of ten concept. If you do, I am confident it will help defeat the stumbling blocks to your falling and safeguard the building blocks to your calling.

> Time flies. It's up to you to be the navigator.
> —Robert Orben

At this point in your life, you may already have a good idea about the purpose and specific calling in your life. You also may be waiting for just the right thing or things to fall in place. Maybe you're thinking, *I just need a bit more experience and time before I start. I need just a little more working capital and resources before I take the plunge. I need just a little more confidence and assuredness before I go full steam ahead. I just need a bit more blah, blah, blah!* Yeah, I know you get the point. If you find yourself drowning in this behavior pattern then I as your friend and advocate implore you to cease and desist.

Don't get me wrong—I'm not saying to just roll the dice and do something foolhardy. What I am saying is to daily transition your position to a life of greatness. Like the steady Eddie Woodpecker, you just keep pecking away, and one day the giant redwood is coming down. You peck away with faith, determination, and persistence that is relentless and never ending. Let the voice that matters and good old-fashioned common sense become the beacon of *light* to the trailblazing of your Purpose PIE® path. Waiting on perfection to fetch your calling is like trying to catch a knife that's falling. Eventually it will be painful and messy. If you continue on this route, you will eventually find yourself right smack dab in the land known as "The Madonna of the Future." This is the title to a story that was written by Henry James. It was about an artist who devoted her entire life to a single painting. But when the artist dies, it is discovered that her canvas is still blank. She never finished because she never started.

> For all sad words of tongue or pen, the saddest are these: "It might have been ..."
> —John Greenleaf Whittier, *Maud Miller*

So how is your "calling" canvas looking these days? Are you filling it with beautiful, perfect imperfections, or is it blank and empty as you wait in vain for perfect expectations? Waiting for perfect conditions will always end up in the junkyard of "it might have been." Waiting for the perfect time and place is a loser's game. Taking action and creating beneficial imperfection is always more meaningful than the most glorious intentional perfection that goes unrealized. So it is imperative that we ACT^3 (Action Creates Traction To Takeoff) on our calling.

> Whoever watches the wind will not plant; Whoever looks at the clouds will not reap. (Ecclesiastes 11:4 NIV)

When we feel that gentle tug of our calling within, we need to be bold and prompt in response to that sacred call to love. We need to carry through with gritty determination and unwavering courage. My last story that I leave with you is a tenderhearted one. It is about a young, dying mother's last two words spoken to her loving son. I see it as a poignant calling to truth and love. It's a moving demonstration of a mother's strong desire to still tenderly nurture her son right up to the very last moment of her life. Just two words spoken, but a library of rich meaning to be mined.

For sixteen years my wife and I lived in Pensacola, Florida. The entire time we were there, I was in the risk management business. Jimmy Holmes was a client of mine and later became, and still is, a dear friend of mine. Every time I was around him, he was always chipper, upbeat, and high on life. One day, however, I sensed that there was something that was deeply wrong and troubling. When I asked him if he was okay, he told me that his mother had recently died. He shared with me that he was at peace with her passing as she was no longer in any pain, but there was one thing that still was filling him with angst. Right before she died, she said two words to him and then repeated them. Those two words were causing emotional heaviness as he was not certain what she was trying to convey to him. Those two words were *be prompt.*

As I started to reflect on that very intimate moment between mother and son, I asked Jimmy to have a seat. Rather quickly I had a strong sensation of what Jimmy's mom was trying to convey. I told him I felt his mom was saying to "be prompt" with anything and everything that was meaningful and significant—to have a keen sense of urgency in fulfilling and completing the truly important things of life; to be reverent to the fragility of life; to be all in and totally present with intentionality to what *really* matters; and to *really live* because it *really* goes by fast! After I shared these thoughts and more, it appeared that a peace came over Jimmy. He seemed more relaxed and settled. It was if I was witnessing a beautiful healing process right before my eyes.

A few years later my wife and I moved to Jupiter, Florida. Shortly after this move my emotional and spiritual dance with songwriting began. After my first song (Purpose PIE®) was completed, I felt compelled to reach out to Jimmy. I called him one day and told him I was going to write a song in tribute to the unique love story between himself and his mother. The song would naturally be entitled, "Be Prompt."

Because this was just the second song I had written, it exudes in perfect imperfections. In spite of this vulnerable fact, I still entered it in the "Song of the Year" international songwriting contest and was shocked when I received their runner-up placement award. Remember, playing out one's purpose and calling in life has absolutely *nothing* to do with perfection. It's all about stumbling forward and operating from the spirit of the deepest place within your heart and being perfectly okay with exposing your creative underbelly to total vulnerability. It's about sensing fear of the unknown, but listening to that gentle whisper within and moving forward anyway. And when you think about it, if we didn't stumble every so often, we certainly wouldn't need or depend on God nearly as much. That certainly would not be in our best interest, for when we depend daily on God, then He empowers us to be prompt to *really* live in the sweet spot of what truly matters.

Be Prompt
Lyrics by Steve Douglas

I'll never forget that cloudy spring day
When my friend stopped by to share and say
That his mama just died and her spirit went away

As I looked at him, I sensed the pain inside
From the quiver of his lips to the mist in his eyes

As we hugged, I said, "Why don't you sit for a while?"
Then he looked at me with a half-hearted smile

He seemed so lost and broken too
So I asked him as a friend what could I do?

He told me as he stood by his mama's side
Holding her hand and loving her so
That her last two words he just didn't know
And all his empty feelings began to show

"Be prompt, be prompt," that's what she said
And these two words just troubled him so
As I looked at my friend, I told him, "These words are a gift to you!
You see, life has a way of sneaking up on you
And before you know it, it will fly by too!"

So be prompt, be prompt, that's what she said
And in those words I can hear her say
Don't dilly-dally or lolly-gag
'Cause your dreams will become as worthless
As a wet paper bag. Yes they will!

So be prompt, be prompt, that's what she said
And in those words I can hear her say
Don't you tarry or delay
When you have sunshine you better make hay!
Yes, you had!

So be prompt, be prompt, that's what she said
And in those words I can hear her say

Get off your duff and quit dragging your feet
'Cause its goals with action that makes life sweet!
Yes, they are!

So be prompt, be prompt, that's what she said
And in those words I can hear her say
Don't you catch that emotional disease
Of could-a, should-a, would-a. Just spare me the drama
If you please!

So be prompt, be prompt, that's what she said
And in those words I can hear her say
Don't get caught on someday... *I'll*
'Cause words are cheap
But a promise to your mama, that you should keep
On your life's bucket list. Don't you forget
To have some fun!
But above all else just get it done!

And with those words, my friend got up to go
He thanked me for my time, and said, "Now I know!
I'll never spend another day like it's one thin dime
'Cause each and every moment is so divine
Now that I own that inner chime."

Of be prompt, be prompt, that's what he said
And in those words as he walked away
I could hear him say
Yesterday's history, tomorrow's a mystery
All we ever have is today
Now I see why they say

Today is called the present, 'cause it's a gift
Now I know what my mama meant
When she gazed at me as her life was spent
And whispered these words on her dying breath

Be prompt, be prompt, that's what she said
Be prompt, be prompt, that's what she said

I've shared with you what I feel are the necessary ingredients in discovering and fulfilling your purpose and specifically designed calling in life. I've listed my personal recipe of how I found my daily slice to the sweet spot of life. I now want to encourage you to be prompt in doing the same. Now is the time to ACT^3 in creating your very own one-of-a-kind Purpose PIE® extravaganza! And when you do, you will ultimately discover what I did.

If I were allowed only one word to describe the Purpose PIE® journey, then that one word would be *love*. When you start to play out your true, unique, and authentic calling, you will find that this process of maturing your soul has love written all over it. You will blossom into a deep and abiding love for God and others that you didn't know existed. And when your love takes flight so effortlessly and generously, you will experience a boomerang of blessings that will take your breath away. You will then know what a Purpose PIE® high is all about. In that very moment you will know that you've come home for the first and last time. Life is all about time, and we only have so much of it. Now it is your time to have the time of your life! So be bold. Be prompt. Be *all* that God intended you to be!

Epilogue

One of the many things I discovered from the Purpose PIE® journey is that we have far more radiant magnificence within our beings than we can possibly imagine. But far too many miss this glorious adventure by not welcoming their sacred Light to shine within. When we are in disconnect with our Inner Voice many times our world takes on a shade of gloomy gray. When we choose to place our emotional welcome mat out daily to our Inner Voice, then our world becomes filled with vibrant color.

The colors for the cover for Purpose PIE® were intentional and not selected at random. I thought you might like to know why.

Blue- Is often associated with depth and stability. Since our true purpose comes from God and there is nothing deeper or more stable than God, then Blue seemed the appropriate color for Purpose. It also symbolizes trust, loyalty, wisdom, confidence, intelligence, faith, truth and heaven. What else can I say!

Red- This color was selected for the P in passion because red is associated with energy, strength, power, determination as well as passion, desire and love.

Yellow- Was chosen for the I in inspiration as yellow is the color of sunshine and associated with joy, intellect and energy. This makes sense when you reflect on inspiration from God (to breathe life into another).

Orange- This was the perfect match for the E in enthusiasm as orange represents enthusiasm, as well as fascination, creativity, determination and success.

Another point of interest: When Purpose PIE® was in its infancy, it started with an acronym (PIE) and carried through the creative process with many acronyms thereafter. Almost all of these would present themselves when awakening in the night and BAM! There they were in my mind, out of nowhere. I would get out of bed, write it down and then try to go back to sleep. By the way: the first letter of Chapters 3-13 creates the acronym INGREDIENTS! So whether you are making an edible pie or creating a Purpose PIE® you need certain ingredients to put in, in order to get something special and beautiful out of it. And herein lies a great truth. No matter what you put in your Purpose PIE® quest, God will always give you back *more*. He will give you the *more* you have been searching for, and then some. Then you will have come home to the sweet spot of *really* living, back into the loving arms of God.

Acknowledgements

First and foremost, I want to thank the two people that have had the greatest influence and impact in my life. My wife and my mother. Their steadfast faith, unwavering support, and encouragement of me carrying out God's calling has been both deeply moving and inspiring beyond measure.

I would like to thank Brian Tracy for his kind words in validating the Purpose Pie message, as he demonstrated the noble art of paying it forward.

And a heartfelt thank you to all the kind and talented people at WestBow Press that have professionally assisted me in bringing about Purpose PIE®, in affording me the opportunity to share it with the world.

Printed in the United States
By Bookmasters